THE PRIVILEGED ADOLESCENT

A. D. G. GUNN

M.R.C.S., L.R.C.P., M.R.C.G.P., D.Obst.R.C.O.G., D.P.H.

THE
PRIVILEGED
ADOLESCENT

*An outline of the physical and mental problems
of the student society*

MTP

Medical and Technical Publishing Co Ltd
Chiltern House, Aylesbury

PUBLISHED BY MTP,
MEDICAL AND TECHNICAL PUBLISHING CO. LTD.
CHILTERN HOUSE, OXFORD ROAD, AYLESBURY, BUCKS.

SBN 85200 005 7

FIRST PUBLISHED 1970

PRINTED IN GREAT BRITAIN BY
BILLING & SONS LIMITED
GUILDFORD AND LONDON

Contents

Foreword

ADOLESCENCE is an artificial state, created by the demands of complex modern society for further education. Youth is prolonged by the requirements of training, apprenticeship, school, college and university, and those who are better intellectually endowed than others face a time of further education that may last from at least three to six years after leaving school. As such they are privileged by the opportunities they can enjoy–and the student who belongs to the educational élite of today can belong to the social élite of tomorrow's world. These privileged adolescents, however, have much need of understanding, sympathy, and help through the crises of development, be they social, psychological or environmental in cause–because the student of today is the most precious investment for the community's future. Whether it be problems of academic wastage, stress, depression, adjustment to personal relationships or the demands of just simply growing up, the privileged adolescent has a difficult time in contemporary society. If we, as parents, doctors, teachers, taxpayers and adults are responsible for making it any more difficult than it ought to be, by prejudice, lack of understanding or through not offering the right help at the right time, then we bear a terrible responsibility. Society will suffer for the harm it causes its adolescents and there are many who feel, perhaps justifiably, that addiction, promiscuity, suicide, depression and neurosis are symptoms of 'social illness' marked out by individual tragedy.If this book helps anyone to understand better the problems faced by the privileged adolescent, then it will have achieved its purpose and perhaps in some way helped to prevent, somewhere, the ignorance and prejudice that leads to conflict. The generation gap is not that of time, social change or modern fashion, it is that of communication.

ALEXANDER D. G. GUNN

Reading, Berkshire

April 1970

CHAPTER ONE

The Numbers

'Higher education (academic, professional, technological and artistic) is provided in institutions such as universities and colleges for which (*a*) the basic requirement is completion of secondary education, (*b*) the usual entrance age is 18 and (*c*) the course leads to the giving of a named award.'
– definition by UNESCO World Survey of Education

THROUGHOUT the world there are more than 50,000,000 young people between the ages of 17 and 21 pursuing tertiary education. They are the new champions in their society, perhaps at times vociferous in their discontent, and looked upon with ambivalent feelings of anxiety or envy by their elders, but certainly they represent a most precious investment for they are the privileged twentieth-century 'apprentices' who will become the managers, administrators, professionals and teachers of the future. They are the new class of the 'classless society' for they are educationally and intellectually the élite.

Universally, the pattern of tertiary education is changing dramatically in response to the needs of a society that is becoming evermore sophisticated technologically. In the United Kingdom, in the past forty years the number of full universities has trebled. Whereas before the 1914–18 war under 1 per cent of young people attended a university, nowadays the proportion is nearer 7 per cent and within the next decade this will rise to 10 per cent. In the United States,

45·6 per cent of males aged 18–19 and 29·2 per cent of females of the same age have remained at school undergoing formal education with a view to acceptance into higher institutions of learning, but the adolescents of lower socio-economic status 'drop out' as they marry, get jobs or enter the armed forces. In Europe it is clear that the number of students enrolled for higher education has increased considerably and annually since the end of World War II. Moreover, since 1945, 1,200 million people have radically changed their form of government and 800 million have achieved political independence. They are demanding opportunities for higher education and their governments are requiring more and more highly qualified personnel to fill new positions in their society. There has been an international rise in the birth rate and–of more impact still–a greater degree of survival of the child to adolescence and adulthood due to the advances of medicine and environmental control. The result is that, for the world as a whole, between 1930 and 1960 the number of students trebled. In Europe the greatest increases have been in Turkey, Yugoslavia, the Federal Republic of Germany and the USSR– the latter having an average increment of 15 per cent per year in the number of students undertaking formal tertiary university or technological education.

In almost every country of the world, therefore, greater numbers of young adolescents are having their education prolonged. In terms of productivity and contribution to the economy of their country they are, during this period of their lives, making a negative contribution. They need supporting, financing and supplying with all the facilities necessary (from capital expenditure on buildings to maintenance services and academic staffing). Prolonged education is not cheap. The needs, too, of further and further extension by post-graduate education creates a group in the community who will not be in employment until the age of 24–25. They are fully-grown mature adults, often married with families, who have not made any obvious material contributions to society until after a third of their life-span has expired. Every country, however, has to make this investment and undertake the responsibility of creating this privilege for those who have shown themselves capable of benefiting, because in the long run, in the course of decades rather than years, it is an investment which no nation can afford to overlook.

The tremendous increase in the number of those undergoing higher education is, moreover, not merely a question of natural population increase, but a genuine increase in the proportion. In the USSR per 100,000 of the population at all ages, 1,041 are students; in the USA, 970; in the Netherlands, 769; Poland, 571; Czechoslovakia, 563; and all the other European countries have rates above 400. The older universities of Europe and America are also undertaking the education of more students from the developing countries of other continents as greater degrees of international co-operation are brought about by such organisations as UNESCO, the World Health Organisation and Fellowship and Scholarship Foundations.

Host country	Percentage of 'foreign' students to 'native' student population
Switzerland	32·3
Austria	25·0
USSR	24·0
USA	23·4
Ireland	22·8
France	11·1
United Kingdom	10·0
Federal Republic of Germany	7·3

Whilst any rate of growth in the number of students undertaking tertiary education is related inevitably to the birth rate some two decades earlier, nevertheless by far the most important influence in determining the number of applications for universities and for other types of higher education is the number of people who achieve the minimum academic qualification for admission. This number, both absolutely and as a proportion of the age-group 17–23, has steadily risen throughout the developed nations. In 1953 there were 80,602 students in British universities, by 1959 the number was 104,009. Ten years later it had increased to 212,000, and as we enter the seventies the number has risen to over a quarter of a million. Thus in the fifties the universities grew by about a quarter in terms of student numbers, whilst in the sixties they doubled. This huge increase probably represents the results of the developing methods of primary and secondary education particularly in societies where all education up to the age of 16 is free.

Thus we have increases in the total number, increases in the proportion of the population, and increases in the numbers of overseas–originating adolescents who are undertaking further education. It is not surprising, therefore, that because of this the 'student' in modern society is more prominent, more noticed and receives an ever-increasing proportion of attention from the community and its media of communication. They are still a minority group but there are more of them. More families have one, or know one, than in any previous generation. This inevitably affects the attitude of the older generation, who expect the student still to be somewhat special, exceptionally gifted, and of a far superior talent to themselves – judgements based on their own experience of life. The seeds of conflict are sown by rapid changes in society – and by changes of the very sort that are being seen in the pattern of extended education for the young.

Tertiary education has altered in a far wider context in the last two decades than just in terms of numbers. In the United Kingdom, for example, the colleges of education, which provide the major source of teachers for the country, have quadrupled their intake. Technical colleges have over 70,000 full-time students, and part-time further education in terms of day-release, evening classes and voluntary further learning cater for more than half a million students over the age of 18. There are those who have left school and sought employment but still wish to avail themselves of courses that lead to some sort of advanced qualification. In a very real sense they are a true part of the student body. Similarly the courses and facilities offered have achieved a new diversity, with well over 500 subjects available for the student who wishes to enrol at the British universities.

There has been, too, an interesting evolutionary pattern in the development of the institutions of higher education. The ivy-clad walls of the older universities have been progressively surrounded by extensions in glass and concrete, and the newer institutions have mushroomed in nearly every major town or its vicinity. The technical colleges have grown unrecognisably until they have in many places surpassed in size, importance and budget many of the older educational institutes – one has only to think of the Massachusetts Institute of Technology or the University of Manchester's Institute of Science and Technology to appreciate this. The demands for specialised and almost prohibitively expensive equipment in the study of scientific disciplines such as sophisticated computers, linear accelerators or radio telescopes, for example, has meant that in particular countries there are certain institutions which command both international respect and a pressing national demand from those who wish to study the particular speciality for which that institution has a reputation. These institutions then benefit from the academic snowball of attracting and being able therefore to select the best staff, and hence the best students, and so increase in size as their undergraduate and post-graduate numbers rise. Geographical factors play their part in the development of marine engineering, and marine biology departments, textile engineering and aeronautics faculties grow near areas where these industries flourish. Internationally there is a new and growing demand by the young to study the subjects of social science such as psychology, sociology and a tendency to desert the pure unapplied sciences, all of which is having its effect on the evolution of tertiary education institutes.

In the United Kingdom, particularly, *l'explosion scolaire* has been largely ingnited by the system of State subsidy. Fifty years ago money for maintenance and development came overwhelmingly from sources other than the central government–mainly income from endowments, benefactions from individuals and private bodies, and fees paid by students. Likewise the majority of students were financed wholly by their families or by their own efforts. Today the State, through the University Grants Committee, overshadows all other sources of finance, contributing close on 90 per cent of the ordinary income of university institutions as a whole; and there has been in consequence a growth of State support for students–leading to a situation where nowadays virtually no aspirant to a university education in the United Kingdom is excluded by lack of money. This situation is closely paralleled by the majority of the European countries, whilst in the United States the society is able to make its contribution by helping the lower socio-economic class of students to 'work their way through'. The élite who are students are no longer those who of necessity in the past had to come from a class whose parents could afford to support them.

There are many effects on the community of all these changes. Greater numbers make the students a more obvious proportion of the community, greater size of the institution means that few in any town can ignore or be unaware of its existence. Being a larger proportion of the community and representing a more heterogeneous socio-economic background grants the student a certain *élan* and distinction that is totally new to society. Without tradition, larger and larger numbers of our youth must undertake this *rite de passage*, and fulfil the initiation rights demanded by a technological society in getting their degree or qualification–before they can assume the role in adult life that their intellectual ability has destined them for. Parents are anxious for them to achieve the status of being 'a student', yet the social attitudes of young people today are in a state of flux, particularly in the direction of increasing independence from family ties. For the overseas student the home country's need for an academic élite weighs heavily as a responsibility, for graduation may be regarded as a matter of local or even national prestige, yet their experience abroad may lead to their earnest desire to return home and radically change the society from which they came. In the midst of State-subsidised educational affluence the student of today would seem to be developing an exceptional concern for others who are less privileged socially and politically, and shows at the same time a high disregard for possessions; like latter-day puritans pursing their lips at their materialistic elders.

There are profound social, academic, economic and numerical changes taking place in further education as part of the continued revolution that science, technology and almost every aspect of modern developed society has produced in our lives. Not the least of these changes has been the obvious complications that have arisen from rapid social transition for young persons who are, after all, still in the later stages of physical and psychological adolescence. The effects of their studies and attendant stresses, the ability that is latent in every institution to be harmful in some degree to its members, the essentially temporary status and insecurity of their lives as students, the personal identity crises and needs for adaptation to new learning methods, and the conflict between dependency and rebellion are all apparent to those who follow the profession of caring for the health of this new – and vulnerable – group of society. The adolescent of today who is a student is indeed privileged – as no other youth of previous generations has been, in terms of numbers, opportunity and facility for further education – but then there is a price to pay for this privilege. A price paid by the community, the parents, and the students themselves – a toll that can be seen not just in terms of money, taxes and economic delays of earning power,

but one extracted in emotional conflict, motivational difficulties, psychological upset and simple physical health. To understand the problems of the privileged adolescent may help to reduce this toll.

Bibliography and Further Reading

Barnard, J. (1961), Ann. Amer. Acad. Polit. and Social Science, November, 1.

Caine, Sir Sidney (1969), *British Universities: Purpose and Prospects*, Bodley Head, London.

Fleming, C. M. (1963), *Adolescence and its Social Psychology*, Routledge & Kegan Paul, London.

Garrison, K. C. (1965), *The Psychology of Adolescence*, Prentice-Hall, New Jersey.

World Health Organisation (1966), Technical Report Series, 320.

University Grants Committee (1968), *Enquiry into Student Progress*, HMSO, London.

UNESCO (1966), World Survey of Education IV, Higher Education, Paris.

Vaisey, J. (1969), *New Statesman*, October 17, 527.

CHAPTER TWO

Adolescent Development

WHAT is an adolescent—in terms of physical and psychological development? In primitive communities, the definition is relatively easy, because the 'stage' of adolescence as we know it is virtually non-existent; there is only pre-puberty, puberty and adulthood, with the rubicon form one to the other being passed as soon as either—male or female—reaches the physically mature stage of being able to procreate. In the developed society it is all, however, prolonged by the demands of education, and is characterised by a stage where the individual is neither a child nor an adult and is recognised as neither by all the other members of society who are older or younger. The stage is given a name, based often in the past on the mode of dress adopted by those who are in this somewhat unfortunate group—the 'flappers', 'bobby-soxers', 'teen-agers', 'teddy boys', 'mods' or 'rockers', 'hippies'—and there are perhaps subtle connotations of disrespect in most of these terms that are used by the mass-media of communication for the sake of brevity. 'Student' has lately become a term which in newspaper headlines tends to infer automatic hirsutism, drugs, protest and promiscuity, and it is as if even informed society cannot free itself of the desire to categorise and tar all our developing youth with the same brush. The interesting point is that in medical terms it is impossible to define adolescence; even in psychological terms attempts at definition become epigramatic rather than precise. Some have said, for example, that an adolescent is 'someone who, when

B   17

treated as an adult, behaves as a child', others that adolescence is 'a process of adaptation to puberty', but in the long run any classification must be sociological, not medical or psychological, for the group's characteristics vary from culture to culture. In the UK it is possible that the recent lowering of the statutory age of responsibility and right to vote to 18 (from 21) will affect the legal attitude to adolescence, but society has not fully committed itself for 21 remains the age for family celebration, and is still the minimum age at which one may enter Parliament. The confusion is overall – legally, physiologically and socially – and this is in fact the hall-mark of the group, for it is a stage, that is drawn out over several years, of maturation and evolution – physically, psychologically and socially – from childhood to adulthood.

In physical terms the adolescent is a growing organism. The influence exerted by the hormones of the body begins with the earliest hidden changes in endocrine activity that initiate the secondary sexual characteristics and it continues until sexual and physical development are complete. The peculiar behaviour of the adolescent in the adults' eyes, which some find irritating, infuriating or incomprehensible is a lot easier to tolerate if one studies the profound changes which are taking place in the physical and mental spheres during this period.

Procreative ability is being achieved physiologically at the cost of the menarche for girls and seminal emissions for the boys. The appearance of pubic hair in the axilla and the groin, the acceleration of skeletal growth demonstrated by height and the increase in muscularity with a radical rearrangement of the disposition of body-fat are the stamp of the early hormonal alternations. In terms of the human animal's growth curve, it is fastest at birth and immediately after, followed by a gradual slowing until the years of adolescence when the curve spurts to a peak comparable with the magnitude of the rate of that of a two-year old. In the male this is accompanied by a great increase in muscularity, and if strength is measured throughout childhood at six-month intervals it will be seen to double itself within each two years of the early stages of adolescence. Girls show this same spurt two years earlier than boys and are thus physically more mature than boys throughout this development period. This difference is most important, for psychological development is inevitably tied most closely to physical maturation.

In terms of precise physical change there is a wide range in the age at which any statistical standards are achieved. For instance, the range for the start of accelerated penile growth is from 11–15, with an average of 13, and for the end of this growth period it is $13\frac{1}{2}$–$18\frac{1}{2}$ with an average of 15. In considering the onset of menstruation, the girl shows the constant recurring pattern of completing her various phases of development in advance of her male contemporary. This pattern is the same throughout the range of primates—the female is always ahead in development, even at birth. Bone development is earlier and so is the onset of sexual change *but* then she stops two years before the male, one of the major sex differences. The age of the menarche is now around 13·01 years in the UK, and the current range is 1–2 years either side of this average. The girl at the same time is undergoing a period of rapid growth in height and in the width of hips. Breast development takes place, but despite the onset of menstruation there is evidence to show that it is at least a year after the menarche before regular ovulation occurs. The earlier the menstrual onset, however, the greater is the tendency towards a more 'feminine' adult body structure in later life than those with a late onset. In a study, for example, undertaken on 300 adult nurses of ages from 20–37, it was clearly shown that there were significant differences in height and fat distribution that correlated with the adult pattern between the early developers who were more 'standard', and the late who were less so. The age of onset, therefore, of secondary sexual development, particularly in the female, will show its effects throughout later adult life; the later starter remains 'late'. Evidence from physical examinations on adopting couples demonstrates clearly that late menstrual onset is associated with varying degress of subsequent infertility, and the particularly late developer therefore may be somewhat handicapped throughout the rest of her life.

There is, for both sexes, a marked change in the structure of the skin and the activity of the skin glands. The delicate soft skin of the child becomes coarser, the pores enlarge and hirsutism becomes more prominent. The sweat glands in the axilla secrete a more fatty and odourous sweat, and with girls there are distinct cyclical changes in the skin with the menstrual variation. The sebaceous glands of the skin respond to the varying balance of growth hormone and secondary sexual hormones by activity that leads invariably to the appearance of 'blackheads' on the face, shoulders and chest wherever they are blocked and the sebum is oxidised. The facial hair on the male thickens, darkens and grows, necessitating shaving by the age of 15–16, whilst development of axillary and pubic hair is completed and hair on the limbs and chest follows in its appearance. The late development feature is the wedge-shaped recess at either side of the upper hair-line on the forehead of the male and achievement of adult testicular volume, and for the female the adult contour of the breast is finally achieved in the late teens.

Of practical interest to the physician is the evidence that haemoglobin level (a measure of the oxygen-carrying capacity of the blood) rises with sexual maturity in the male and not in the female, but for both sexes the blood pressure is also a function of the stage of development, and this rises as the adult physique is achieved. Dental changes are occurring throughout this period, and again the female is in the advance of the species, but the eruption of the 'wisdom' teeth marks the completion of this stage.

There are some extremely important points to note in even so brief a discussion of the physical changes that take place in adolescence and they are as follows:

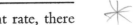

(1) Individuals grow and develop at a different rate, there are no categorial 'norms'.
(2) Profound social and cultural differences are seen, probably as a result of a combination of genetic, racial, and economic factors.
(3) The psychological maturation of the individual is directly affected by the stage of physical development.
(4) There is a tendency in the highly developed countries for an earlier achievement of most of the growth stages by the present generation than with previous ones, and this trend is continuing.

Not only are there sex differences in all forms of physical development but a broad range of the age of achievement for each sex. As wide a range in fact as 4–5 years, and for some individuals there is a wide range of the speed at which developmental stages are achieved and passed through–some boys may go through a penile growth stage in three years, others in five; some girls regularly menstruate from the onset of the menarche, others have grossly irregular cycles for as long as four or five years. The significance of this is that any doctor, teacher or parent may have in the practice, class or family adolescents who may be of a particular age but nevertheless are at a quite different stage of physical development from that of their contemporaries or from that at which their siblings were when they were that age. This is not always appreciated, and to grade adolescents by precise ages is physically and psychologically meaningless. In a class of 15-year-olds some girls will be fully sexually aware and developed, others will be still pre-pubescent–with boys the physically developed will be separated at the same age in any group by their physique, attitude of mind and social behaviour, from those who are not.

The cultural, racial and economic differences are also important. It is held that adequate nutrition throughout childhood determines the earlier onset and completion of development in the adolescent and there is considerable evidence to support this contention. An example of this is a survey by Burrell (50,000 participants). In the West Indies the menarche occurs

Distribution of age at menarche of Bantu girls from poor and comparatively wealthy homes:

	10%	25%	50%	75%	90%
Age in years (poor)	13·6	14·5	15·4	16·3	17·2
Age in years (wealthy)	13·4	14·2	15·2	15·8	16·6

among Negroes significantly later than it does among the better off and better-fed Negro in the United States. But racial differences also play their part despite nutritional advantages, and these were clearly demonstrated in the work of Ellis (1,000 participants), where the Nigerian schoolboys represented a 'select' group of their own community and comparable in many ways in their standard of living to those in the UK. Thus Burrell's and Ellis's work demonstrated that, given firstly the same racial groups, standards of nutrition – if good – ensured earlier development; but that given comparable standards and different ethnic backgrounds development would still follow the genetic and racial patterns. These differences are again important for any adult involved in the care of, or contact with, a mixed ethnic or social group of adolescents. Teachers, for example, will find it particularly difficult to initiate and control sex and hygiene instruction when dealing with any group of children above the age of 11, because of all these profound differences of age development, ethnic maturation patterns and socio-economic factors that have rendered their class heterogeneous sexually and physically.

By far the most important feature of adolescent development is the fact that psychological and therefore social maturation depends on the physical development of the individual. There is a very close interrelation, so much so that severe psychological upset will in fact inhibit growth during adoles-

PUBESCENCE IN NIGERIAN SCHOOLBOYS
COMPARED TO THAT OF A CONTROL GROUP
IN GREAT BRITAIN

| | Per cent pubescent* | |
Age group	Nigeria	Great Britain
9–10	6·0	0·0
10–11	6·5	5·0
11–12	21·1	13·5
12–13	40·8	35·8
13–14	38·9	43·7
14–15	48·5	39·2
15–16	18·7	29·5
16–17	16·7	18·2
17–18	0·0	11·4

* The sum of the per cents for each group is more than 100, since the period of pubescence includes a period of more than one year for most of the boys. Thus, many boys are counted more than once. The criteria used for grading were: non-pubescent when pigmented pubic hair was entirely absent and genital development infantile; pubescent when pigmented pubic hair and/or early but incomplete genital development was present; and adolescent or post-pubescent when both growth of pubic hair and genital development were advanced.

cence in exactly the same way that emotional upsets are so frequently reflected in almost any adolescent girl's menstrual cycle. Early physically maturing children who attain adult proportions very quickly have obviously a longer period in which to make the social adjustments which are expected of them before entry upon adult responsibilities. They may inevitably, however, pass through a period of considerable loneliness until their contemporaries develop to their level,

but the prestige of such boys and girls is high and they tend to
show greater confidence–as a 'leader group' amongst their
contemporaries–and they establish better personal relationships with adults than their more retarded colleagues. There
are times however when, if one aspect of growth, say height,
precedes the other organic developments, an individual may
experience difficulties because the adult assumes he or she is
more 'grown up' than they are. The expectation by adults of a
greater degree of maturity than the adolescent can display
is one of the major problems of relationships at this age. The
adolescent is aware that his or her body is changing but is
uncertain of the consequent social status. Being still treated
as a child, a subject of 'parental blindness', or suffering from
adult unwillingness to admit the individual as a new fully
grown member of the family circle, are all the sort of experiences the developing youth meets and are major causes of the
friction that arises in the 'generation gap'. In late development
by the adolescent there may be an unwelcome (to the adult)
persistence of infantile attitudes to life. The psychological and
intellectual changes run parallel to the physical development,
and thus late menstruation correlates with late attachments to
the opposite sex, a diminution in the number and extent of
their sexual experiences and also to some degree with sub-
fertility in later life. Californian studies have demonstrated,
for example, a higher neurosis rate and decreased sociability
amongst late developing adolescents.

Intellectually the adolescent has entered a stage of life where
theories of the abstract appeal, where there is a start of the pas-
sion for ideas and ideologies, and where the concept of proportions of balance between cause and effect can be appreciated.
It is a new kind of thinking to that of the child, but is untemp-
ered by the experience of the adult. Authorities have claimed
that from the standpoint of psychiatry the adolescent falls
somewhere on the border between mental health and illness.
A person, all of whose organs are mature and functioning, may
be physically healthy, but a person with all mental functions

proceeding well may still be unhealthy if the relationship between them is disturbed. Thus the boy with frequent erections and consequent noctural or manually produced emissions may be in all physical terms in perfect health, but obsessed by guilt and neurotic as a result. Equally the girl who pretends to be of mature sexuality to keep up with her contemporaries may pass through agonising dysmenorrhoea, or prolonged periods of amenorrhoea, and either not be prepared to admit it or else become an obsessional physician-consultor as a result of her feelings that all below the navel is unwell. Drives, ideas and sense of reality may well be perfectly sound in adolescence, but mental health may be upset if the necessary compromise and balance between them is absent. A girl, for example, who is truly promiscuous, may be striving to achieve a feeling of wholeness that matches her physical development, and so if her family or personal background is disturbed she is prone to establish unfortunate personal relationships as substitutes for the stability she needs. Her relationship with a boy may not be with him as a person but as a source of comfort. 'She takes the boy's penis into her vagina as the infant sucks its thumb.' There is a vicious un-happiness for all concerned where the girl's symptom of emotional distress is shown in promiscuity, for her demands made of her boy-friends are 'clinging' and she is rejected be-cause of this, or because of her unstable behaviour. The girl's fears of being rejected are the very reason for her rejection: and to reassure herself she is still a woman she may even try to become deliberately pregnant. An adult would probably be able to develop some insight into their own needs and the dangers of their own behaviour which would cause their automatic modification, but an adolescent is subject to almost overwhelming drives that easily lead to unbalance. There is a genuine effort by most adolescents to keep their drives, desires and fantasies under control, but there are occasional break-throughs punctuating the pattern of continual strain, so that one never knows whether one will meet the restrictive phase or one of the breaks-through of infantile behaviour. Thus liberation from the parents may be accompanied by indifference to them, or a disparagement of them, and attempts to get rid of their influence will alternate with periods of dependence on them. For their part, parents find it difficult at one moment to be self-effacing and non-existent, and at the next to be called on to answer demands as before. Often the closer the earlier tie, the more violent will be the 'fight'.

There is also a considerable 'class' difference in the social attitudes that any adolescent adopts. They may all, as they pass through this evolutionary stage of their lives, be subject to growth variation, to cultural variations and to fashions contemporary to their time, but nevertheless there are certain trends, depending on their socio-economic origins and therefore their childhood influences, which they unconsciously follow. The lower economic-class male may often appear to be uninvolved emotionally with their girls although they may be having intercourse with them. Open aggression may be a feature of their sexual relationships and they may see nothing wrong in brutalising, hitting or abusing her. It is the 'manly' thing not to be 'soft' on a girl. The middle economic-class boys, however, perhaps protected from too frequent social exposure by the family, tend to have intercourse for the first time at a later age than the so-called working-class boys. They are more likely to use contraceptives when they do and to 'care' for the girl and accept a greater degree of responsibility in the relationship and its future. The higher economic classes may have provided a more prolonged family protection environment for their adolescents and so in many cases committed their young to boarding schools. Such prolongation of single environments often produces a degree of social retardation that is marked. It does not lead to homosexuality *per se*, it merely provides an opportunity for its display that is to some extent inevitable. In closed male societies like boarding schools, boys may show a morbid preoccupation with sexuality which they cannot avoid because there are few social outlets for it.

The need for emotional contact can lead to mutual masturbation, especially since the underground language of the boys is so frequently directed towards genital display and subjects associated with sexual behaviour. Physically bigger and better developed boys often teach smaller ones to masturbate, and moreover there is for the smaller ones a need to belong to the 'group'. This no more turns otherwise healthy boys into permanent homosexuals than having a 'crush' on the agile gym mistress turns younger girls into lesbians.

Girls 'compare themselves' in much the same way as boys do, emphasising breast size and the onset of menstruation in the early years, but later their 'coinage' for success evolves round the stories of their heterosexual exploits. A boy is a necessary part of their self-assessment, their testing of each other and themselves and the realisation of feminity—the hall-mark of their maturity in the eyes of their juniors. This can lead to unfortunate situations where the less developed (psychologically) girl feels she must firstly have a boy-friend and secondly experience intercourse. It is the 'done' thing. Amongst students particularly, the feeling that 'to belong' involves a sexual relationship may prove responsible for much unhappiness and maladjustment in personal relationships.

The preoccupation of the adolescent with their bodies is hardly surprising. The physical changes they are witnessing and experiencing are considerable, and their social status in the eyes of their colleagues, parents and adult world is seen to depend on them. Boys who experience a delay are liable to be teased as being 'effeminate', 'weaklings' or rejected by their social peers whom they worship as heroes. Sometimes members of either sex may sublimate their feelings in academic work and score intellectually where they lose physically, thus gaining a considerable degree of satisfaction. Girls may assert themselves in sport, athletics or cloak their insecurity in aggression. Early developers often make themselves gang-leaders—a position they lose when their juniors catch up with them and which they strive to maintain with symbols of leadership and daring that might involve antisocial behaviour. Vandalism and hooliganism often starts as a desire to impress.

It is extremely unfortunate that at this time of great stress the environment makes greater demands on the adolescent in the academic and other fields, for in many ways this could happen at no worse time. The role of aggression–in wartime, on the sportsfield and in deprived societies–fulfils many individual adolescents. If it shows, however, in family and personal relationships, then it can lead to great distress, but it is one of the roles that modern developed society frustrates by demanding 'civilised' conformity to adult standards. Modes of dress, behaviour, language and attitudes adopted by the adolescent constantly reflect the desire to rebel– and yet this is the time in their lives in which we expect them to behave, be a 'credit' to their parents and to wait patiently for the completion of their academic and technological education. Perhaps we expect too much, forget how as youths we felt at their age, and provide too few outlets for natural adventure, enthusiasm and energy. The Battle of Britain was won by those of the same age who now riot in Berkeley, Grosvenor Square, and Tokio–in the World Wars they gave their lives, and now all they seem to give to the adult is trouble. Conformity is not what we should expect, for adolescence is a time of irregular physical development, differing psychological maturity, and seething social torment. Antisocial behaviour by some adolescents may well not be excusable–at least it is, or should be, largely understandable.

Bibliography and Further Reading

Burrell, J. W. et al. (1961), *Human Biology*, 33, 250.
Ellis, R. W. B. (1950), *Brit. med. J.*, **1**, 85.
Faulkner, F. (1960), *Child Dev., An International Method of Study*, Basel, Karger.
Faust, M. S. (1960), *Child Dev.*, 31, 173.
Hubble, D. (1966), *Clin. Paediat.*, 5, 410.

Humphrey, M. H. (1969), *The Hostage Seekers*, Longman, London.

Jacobsen, L. (1954), *Human Biology*, 26, 127.

Kinsey, A. C. *et al.* (1953), *Sexual Behaviour in the Human Male and Female*, Saunders, Philadelphia.

Miller, D. H. (1969), *The Age Between*, Cornmarket–Hutchinson, London.

Mussen, P. H., and Jones, M. C. (1958), *Child Dev.*, 29, 61.

Stanley-Hall, G. (1922), *Atlantic Monthly*, 129, 771.

Tanner, J. M. (1961), *Education and Physical Growth*, University of London Press, London.

—— (1968), *Biological Aspects of Development*, Proc. Brit. Stud. Health. Assn.

Wagner, G. (1961), *The New Outlook*, 55, 299.

CHAPTER THREE

Sex on the Campus

IN TERMS of physical maturity a student is in general no different from his or her contemporaries who are less academically endowed. In terms of emotional maturity, however, the picture may be very different.

'Academic' adolescence is an artificial state—where denied the responsibilities of adulthood, looked upon by parents and the community in general as not-quite-grown-up schoolchildren and yet expected to behave in a manner acceptable to the adult—students are suspended and dependent economically, but a prey to the perfectly normal desires to mate, explore their sexuality and form stable personal relationships. Their contemporaries who left school two years before them already have their wives and husbands, their homes, first cars and perhaps first children—whilst they have only a beard or beads, a lot of books and 'good prospects' to show for their years.

The girl student is perhaps even more at risk to the normal desires for settling down because we have not yet developed a fully emancipated attitude to the female sex (except perhaps in the USSR, where nearly 50 per cent of all students are female) and her criteria of success in later life will include a husband with a good job. She might not see the university as a 'marriage market', but nevertheless subconsciously she will be aware of the fact that once she leaves she will meet fewer intellectual equals and her 'choice' will be more limited. Thus, in the final years of her course, there is an inevitable and sudden sprouting of engagement rings and relationships become more stable. There are many group pressures at work in the field of sex for the student, and the older generation—denied in their lives any similar time, freedom and affluence, as well as the opportunity—find the young person's attitude to sex difficult to understand, or else views it with a mixture of envy, anxiety and foreboding.

It is fair to point out that, interestingly enough, when the student first goes to the university or college his sexual experience and indeed knowledge is demonstrably more limited than that of his contemporaries. This pattern of sexual backwardness is surprisingly being maintained, despite many changes and although there is nowadays a progressive reduction in the age of both physical maturity and sexual experience. One particular investigation of the extent of sexual experience of all social and academic grades of unmarried youth was carried out by interviewing, over a period of three years, 934 boys and 939 girls aged 15–19, from seven differing social and economic areas. The declared object was to collect facts about the sexual attitudes and behaviour of young people and to identify some of the sociological and psychological factors concerned. The exploration of this field is particularly important since it represents the cultural background from which any student may be drawn. The results of this work show not only an interesting contrast with the currently available material that refers to the student community, but also clearly demonstrate the attitudes of the culture group that is common to all contemporary adolescents. Certain differences from the past were noted, including signs of the often-referred-to alienation between the young of today and the adult generations. The increased economic power of teenagers also attracted a good deal of attention because it is concentrated on certain areas of the market which include products that are highly visible and audible, and because their spending power has attracted considerable commercial exploitation. The communication media, of press, TV and radio, have tended in recent years to create a 'teenage mythology'. Boys and girls who do not conform to the publicised pattern begin to feel they are somehow deficient, and thus there is a clearly recognisable 'group' situation which affects every individual adolescent's reaction to sex.

From this report (Schofield) it transpired that by the age of 17, 11 per cent of all boys and 6 per cent of girls had experienced sexual intercourse at least once. By the age of 19 this had risen to 30 per cent and 16 per cent respectively. With regard to the physical exploration of each other's bodies, that had involved at least some degree of undressing, by the age of 17, 60 per cent of boys and 51 per cent of girls in contemporary society had taken part in such activities. It was widely held by the participants of the survey that some of the activities were determined by group pressures, the desire to be thought 'experienced' and to prove masculinity, and among girls the fear of losing a prized friendship. The most usual restraining influence for girls, and an important one for boys, was moral or religious training, but fear of pregnancy was also an important inhibiting factor. Fear of venereal disease seemed to be of small importance. It is interesting to note that we are in days of apparent individual freedom with adequate and safe fertility control becoming continually more easy of access, and yet youth is still subject to a morality based on fear – the fear of not conforming, and the fear of pregnancy. Where these have been rejected by the young people of today (e.g. 'hippy cults') we have a new morality which the older generation cannot understand – because they in their turn were subjected to the same standard fears a generation ago and were unable to reject them.

Knowledge about sex seems to be almost invariably acquired from friends – and often through the medium of 'jokes'. Though 27 per cent of the girls had received information from their mothers, very few boys had done so, and the part of fathers in giving information seemed to be negligible. Middle-class children are found to be more likely to have learnt from their parents than those of a lower socio-economic group, but even so 67 per cent of sons and 29 per cent of daughters of middle-class families in this report had had no advice about sex from their parents. At school 85 per cent of girls but only 47 per cent of boys had received some kind of formal sex education, but this was mainly in the form of biological information. Of equal interest was the fact that 84 per cent of boys and a similar proportion of girls claimed to have know-ledge of contraception, and yet of those with sexual experience less than half the boys and only one girl in five always used some method of birth control. A paradox which is never-theless in keeping with the actual facts concerning the expe-rience, for in the teenage years sex is more often unpredictable than pre-meditated and explorative rather than mutually decided. At least the 'first time' is.

Similar surveys carried out in the United States have defined the sources of knowledge about sex gained by adoles-cents, and they show a striking correlation with the report published from European cultures. For example, was data obtained from 2,000 boys attending Catholic high schools about where they received their first information about sex and from what source or sources they had received subsequent information on this subject. The results revealed that fathers and mothers—as a source—ranked fifth and sixth respectively among the sources from which these boys received their first information. Over one half of the boys received their first knowledge from companions and 34·6 per cent obtained theirs from the 'street'. Results from other studies show that girls, even those from the lower cultural classes, receive their informa-tion about sex from parents to a much greater degree than boys, and there is no doubt that the onset of menstruation creates this stronger parent-link for the young girl. In general, how-ever, children and adolescents receive their information about love and marriage mainly from the homes—as one would expect, for even if the facts of sex are not discussed, at least human relationships are. However, even on this subject the modern communication media play their part, for results

C

from a survey of a thousand American families show that TV, other children and films are important sources of information.

Thus we have an adolescent culture that has absorbed its information and developed its attitude to sexual relationships from a combination of sources–few of which might be regarded as unimpeachable. We have a group in our community who, although unmarried, have already experimented (at least one-third of girls and half the boys) with full sexual experience, and we have a larger group who have many times been mutually 'on the brink' but have restricted their activities due to a morality based on either fear or their upbringing. One would expect, medically, to see the effects of this on the birth rate, and indeed illegitimacy rates have been showing an almost international increase, though it must not be forgotten that a large number of babies who are technically illegitimate are born to older married women. Though we say that the rates are rising steeply (and they certainly are in the younger age groups), we find that the pre-marital conception rate in Great Britain represented 14·5 per cent of all live births in 1938, and they are the same today–the difference being that in 1938 a higher proportion (75–80 per cent) married, and now they do not. In general the figure in the UK for children born of unmarried mothers is 7 per cent, but due to the effects of the 1968 Abortion Act and more freely available contraceptive advice, this figure can be expected to fall.

What, then, of the student, who in all other respects apart from his or her academic ability, emerges equally from this social background of cultural influence? Firstly the pregnancy rate for unmarried female students is far lower than the general national average (particularly in the UK) and is running at an almost annually decreasing rate of 3 per cent or less. The marriage rate for undergraduates is far less again than for their contemporaries–but then economic circumstances influence this – despite the fact that generally the age for marriage is dropping. (As an example of this general effect it is fair to point out that in the longest courses–that is medicine–a decade ago only 10–15 per cent of final year medical students in the UK were married at qualification, currently the rate has risen to 50 per cent.) Despite the general free availability of contraceptive advice from University Health Services, for example, throughout the United Kingdom, when statistics are collated it is found that the highest percentage of girls who are regular oral contraceptive users is less than 15 per cent. The incidence of venereal disease amongst students is minimal (less than 1 per cent), and promiscuity (OED = 'indiscriminate mixture') as by definition girls who cohabit with more than one partner in, say, any one year, is again less than 1 per cent. Indeed, promiscuity in the sense of the girl who 'sleeps around' is seen by university physicians as a sign and symptom of psychological disturbance – the girl is invariably, quite severely emotionally disturbed and her sexual behaviour is but one aspect of her illness. If this general pattern of statistics is so different from that of their contemporaries, why is this? Why is the student so apparently 'deprived'?

It is firstly obvious that any youth, devoted to furthering his education, spends less time at leisure than those who are not, and whose time is free once the demands of their wage-earning occupation are met. The opportunities for the academic schoolboy or girl are limited. Their motivations in life are directed to other ends than those portrayed in the mass media, and economically they have less to spend. Their closeness to the home and family is greater, for they probably have developed habits of working at home, and living at home, at least in vacation, and spend more of their time under the direct influence of the family than does, say, their colleague who is 'on the road', perhaps living in an apartment, or who has moved away into the larger town for employment. These are generalisations, but nevertheless they play their part in explaining the relative sexual backwardness of the college student.

In a detailed survey carried out by the author, an attempt was made to define the social and psychological attitudes of those female students who were, in the main, regular users of the 'pill'. Their identification was not difficult since some 90 per cent of the undergraduates were registered for general medical care with one practice, and the purchase of the oral contraceptive requires a physician's prescription. By means of a 'signal' on the patient's record card the 'pill-takers' could be readily identified. In this practice contraceptive advice is readily available and as freely given as, say, advice on the treatment of 'athlete's foot'; and in general the student who asks about birth control is considered as a responsible adult with a need, and not an opportunity for the physicians to moralise or judge the issue, but to advise. The whole subject is discussed openly, often with the girl's sexual partner, and the method of fertility control best suited to the couple is decided upon and dispensed. This preamble is necessary in order to indicate that no constraint is placed on the young student who seeks advice, and the practice enjoys a reputation for this amongst its student practice population.

The first and most significant fact to emerge from this research was that, despite 'open-door' policy, out of an undergraduate and postgraduate population of some 2,000 girls who were in the main between the ages of 18 and 24, only 228 girls were 'on the pill'. Ten per cent could therefore be considered to be the proportion who were having regular predictable intercourse. The numbers who were having irregular sexual relationships, or using other methods of fertility control, could not be assessed, nevertheless this 'pill' group showed some interesting characteritics that support the general picture of sex on the campus described above.

From the final computerised analysis, the student 'on the pill' is seen to come from the upper socio-economic group (44 per cent of them with parents earning £2,000 or more p.a.) and to be living more than 50 miles from their parents' home (72 per cent). 'Broken' marriages amongst the parents are in the minority (12 per cent), whilst previous pregnancy or abortion was only found in 1 per cent of the total number of girls. With regard to the number of sexual partners, 78 per cent had experienced intercourse with less than three males (51 per cent with one only), and 73 per cent stated that given the opportunity they (eventually) would 'like to marry' their present partner. This is hardly in keeping with the myth of the promiscuous student, and the results moreover refer to a complete three-year cross section of the university population.

Only six girls claimed in the questionnaire to have had sexual relations with more than six partners since starting their sexual career, and in view of the expected percentage of severe emotional disturbance in the community this is fewer than might have been predicted. With regard to domicile, it does not seem to make any significant difference as to whether the girl lives in lodgings, hostel or flat as to whether she uses an oral contraceptive or not. The opportunity must be presumed to be equal, regardless of where the girl lives during term-time, for a stable and regular relationship to flourish, especially in view of the fact that the male partner may be able to offer 'suitable' facilities. There is little truth in the fear that if a female student is allowed to live in an unsupervised flat she will veer from the straight and narrow—it will always depend on the girl. Of equal significance is the fact that 62 per cent of the girls' partners were at the same university or 'living nearby' and only 8 per cent were 'home-town' boy-friends. Thus it is fair for parents to assume that a girl going away from home will be likely during her undergraduate years to form a stable and probably permanent relationship with a male colleague of the same institution.

The attitude to marriage reflected in this survey was, however, particularly interesting. 'Given married accommodation, university flats and unaffected grants, would you marry your present partner now?', was one of the questions asked, and the reply was an overwhelming 'No—not yet' (63 per cent). This must be seen as the current attitude of young girls in later adolescence whose feelings are not necessarily as completely conditioned towards setting up a home as their contemporaries who are not students, but who nevertheless are sure of their man.

We have thus a student community which demonstrates less illegitimacy, less marriage, less venereal disease and less overall regular sexual experience than is seen outside the confines of the 'ivory towers'. What is there then that can be said about the exceptions to these general findings?

Pregnancy and Abortion

Firstly, the pregnant student. The results of a ten-year follow-up carried out in a large university of all students who became pregnant during their academic course are typical of physicians' experience in other institutions, and they showed that during that time there were 150 cases known to the university physicians, 66 per cent of which ended in a normal confinement. 30 per cent aborted (fourteen spontaneously, and eight were legally induced on specialist advice), twenty-two of these having been induced without the physician's knowledge or agreement. There was also a progressive drop in the incidence of pregnancy over the time (1961 4·7 per cent, 1964 2·9 per cent, 1967 2 per cent), and because the Health Service had medical records that could be used to compare every aspect of medical 'usage' then it was possible to trace out any obvious differences between the student who became pregnant and the one who did not. It emerged from this study that the pregnant ones were more than twice as likely to have shown earlier signs of emotional or psychological instability than the others, with manifestations of this in a history of anxiety, or depressive illness. Similar studies have shown that the most pregnancy-prone student is the girl doing a general arts course, with poor academic performance and little motivation with a view to a career. There is also a predominant history of a broken family and, in particular, one of desertion by the father of the girl's mother. This can sometimes be seen as a form of sexual suicide committed by the girl where there is a history of her having insisted on her partner not using contraceptive precautions. Deliberate pregnancy, despite the availability of adequate fertility control, is often a mark of severe emotional distress, and it might be seen by some as a desire by the girl to be totally loved and subconsciously to possess something she herself may love—when in her own family she is surrounded by disaster.

The picture for the pregnant student is changing as a result of alterations in abortion legislation, particularly in the UK, and also in Northern Europe, but internationally this is only happening slowly. The availability of termination treatment is variable, and in the UK may depend to a large degree on the liberality of the local area consultant's interpretation of the law. As a result, voluntary agencies have developed to direct young adolescents who are justifiable cases but unable to obtain advice or termination in their own locality to hospitals where their chances of success are greater. This is an invidious situation at present, but it can be expected that as time passes the general effects of the Abortion Act (UK) will be more widely felt. Nevertheless, it must be admitted that where an otherwise fit and healthy student is concerned the pregnancy is one of social inconvenience and is a threat less to her mental and physical health than to her academic future.

This is the situation in the majority of cases and with these it is of equal importance to decide whether there are psychiatric indications for not terminating pregnancy—as to whether there are. Flight from social inconvenience to a discreet abortion is not necessarily in the girl's best interests and one of the safest guidelines is to determine exactly what the girl herself feels she wants to do most. Too often there are parents or a boy-friend pressurising her when fundamentally she would like to marry, bear her child and perhaps ultimately continue her course. The opposite side of the coin is the girl from a broken home, who is, by being at the university, perhaps only fulfilling the academic ambitions of one or other of her separated parents, and is thus poorly motivated. When she gets pregnant, perhaps deliberately, it is a form of academic suicide and a 'cry for emotional help'—she can pose therefore the most difficult of problems to her medical advisers. There is a need for considerable research and follow-up of all these cases in the new social context of legal termination of pregnancy, for invariably those who are involved are left with a sense of having achieved at best a compromise, regardless of the outcome, and the evidence is lacking as to what are the long-term effects of terminating an inconvenient pregnancy.

If termination is not sought by the girl concerned, or is rejected on mature consideration by all involved, then two possibilities remain open to her: marriage or continuing, though unmarried, to her confinement. The latter choice is very rarely chosen, but if it is, then adoption societies are delighted to help (particularly since the baby of a student is one that is easy to place and much sought after in a society where intelligence—even if presumed—is at a premium) and several students in the author's experience have overcome the apparently unsurmountable difficulties of coping with an illegitimate pregnancy, adoption and the continuance of their studies. There is an impression left after dealing with cases like this, however, that the girl never really accepted the fact that she was pregnant and even after parturition showed no interest whatsoever in the child. In order to facilitate this situation in these cases it is always better for the child to go into 'care' as soon after delivery as possible, not be breast-fed, and for its natural mother to have little more to do with it than the signing of forms in a lawyer's office.

The former choice of marriage is not so rare and here there is some considerable degree of encouragement for all concerned. The married students, even with a baby, tend to do academically better than they would singly, or would otherwise have been expected to do. Whether this is because they are truly well adjusted and the pregnancy a genuine accident that only precipitated in time an inevitable and firmly decided upon occurence, it is difficult to know, but the academic facts speak for themselves. Many of these relationships remain stable, the divorce rate (in contrast to the general pattern that is high for low marriage-age groups) is low, and both work performance and academic results benefit. It might be due to better motivation and less time spent in 'the hunt', but a happy, healthy couple with new-born child are by no means unknown in the lists of first-class academic honours.

Promiscuity and Venereal Disease

There has always been and always will be the small minority who deliberately debase the sexual act and themselves by promiscuous behaviour. The strongest of correlations exist between emotional instability and psychological ill-health. The more immature may not be able to accept or appreciate the feeling of responsibility that sex should and can bring, and seek for gratification at a more superficial level. The need to make responsible choices concerning sexual behaviour is made particularly difficult where there is a vast area of social confusion and a pathological need to rebel. They may act out their conflicts with society in a delinquent or aggressive way—frantically trying to disprove their fears of homosexuality or to get their own back for frustrations suffered in childhood. Sexuality is made use of as an expression of neurosis and in terms of meaning their activity has little effect on them emotionally. There is no satisfaction to be had from promiscuity beyond the spinal reflexes (which in the girl's case may not be all that frequent), for real satisfaction is only derived from an emotionally stable relationship. Girls will consult a physician and complain of their promiscuity because it is something they are frightened of and do not enjoy. The boy will give a history of many shallow relationships as part of the story of his depressive illness. Genuine nymphomania is another of the myths modern society has created for itself, for promiscuity is an illness. This is not to state that any girl of 21 may not have had sexual relationships with perhaps two or three men since the age of 17 and not be perfectly healthy emotionally—she may well be so, each one relationship at the time and for its duration having been one of love and affection later to be found as mistaken by one or other of the partners. In the context of current behavioural patterns of late adolescence this might be considered as normal—just as her mother was 'in love' with two or three 'beau's' until she met her husband, and was kissed by them all. The girl of contemporary society can 'go further' if she wishes to, without fear of pregnancy, than her mother could. Society continually confuses promiscuity with pre-marital intercourse.

Venereal disease is one of the prices, however, of plurality in sexual contact, and whilst syphilis is diminishing (except amongst homosexuals), gonorrhoea is increasing in its incidence. This is the pattern in contemporary society where, for example, 27 per cent of all female attendance in the UK for the treatment of gonorrhoea are made by girls under the age of 20. The student community does not escape this, but nevertheless it is by no means common (as low as 1 per cent). Perhaps because its sexual experience is in the main within the confines of its own captive population, it is not possible to say why. However, one important aspect of venereal contagion is nevertheless common amongst sexually experienced students, namely the trichomonas vaginalis infections. The complaint of vaginal discharge is frequent in the University Health Service's clinics and after monilial infections the trichomonas ones are decidedly the most common. Since treatment, to be effective, entails the medication of both partners, it is reassuring to note the ready responsibility of the male student in attending with promptness for his prescription. Experience in practice outside the university is not always similar.

It is interesting to note that this compaint of vaginal discharge is frequently at the first attendance of the girl in which she initiates a discussion of sexual activity. 'Honeymoon' cystitis is another. Both have a degree of 'guilt connotation' to them and once any dam of embarrassment is breached there is a flood of eager questions and a genuine desire for open discussions. The girl will frequently have her boy-friend with her in the waiting room, and enthusiastically asks if he can come in too. This genuine need for information is an expression of the paucity of agencies, reliable sources, and of confidential counselling services available for adolescents in general, for who else can a young couple turn to for advice and help? There is a mutual responsibility seen in the vast majority where the male partner is often more anxious about any side effects of the 'pill' than his girl friend is, because he loves her. There is in general an appalling ignorance about venereal disease and its symptoms, and an equally misplaced confidence about the 'safe' period – with a widespread fear of their parents 'finding out'. The typical pattern is one of advancing sexual exploration leading to the first act of intercourse for both which ends prematurely and in tears or guilt. The boy then makes some immature and half-hearted attempts to 'use something' which results in both partners hating the whole procedure. The girl with worry, more often than with conception, becomes overdue menstrually and then – and only then – do they seek some help. The menstrual period for the fortunate ones eventually comes and they decide together that 'never again' will they go through such agony and torment – and such is a typical couple attending for contraceptive advice. The 'pill' and 'advice' has no contribution to make to increasing the numbers of adolescents who are having intercourse, it only reduces the pregnancy rate. Of the 200 girls who completed the survey referred to earlier, 100 per cent had used 'other contraceptive methods' or tried them before they came along to ask for something more dependable. Modern fertility control has not, interestingly enough, altered the numbers of adolescents who enjoy a full sexual relationship, only made it less likely that they will be forced to reap the results of their wild oats and enabled them instead to live and love each other, and grow up responsible, caring and, in all probability at the end of their academic career, marrying.

To those who are not involved with the care of students,

or who are not in their intimate confidence, myths about sex on the campus have in many ways become modern fantasies of the adult world. Fantasies that are quite unfounded, as facts prove when proper investigation is undertaken.

It is admittedly exceptionally difficult for the older generation to appreciate the sexual stress and strains of a prolonged and artificial adolescence—when they were the same age they were either sublimating their desires in the desperate need to secure economic independence, or else were married. Constantly parents imagine that their daughters or sons, at the age of 20 or 21, are either totally ignorant of sex, or indulging in lustful pursuits that are more often parental imagination than adolescent fact. Communication between parent and offspring on this subject is too frequently non-existent—as indeed it is at the earlier ages in terms of sexual education. Marriage is resisted and parental pressure is invariably brought to bear to prevent it, from the best of motives perhaps, and parents fear constantly that their daughters will turn up pregnant, or their sons be ensnared by some 'scheming girl'. The facts disprove these fears. Indeed, if more open discussion, confidence and trust could be found in the home, many of the adolescents' stresses and strains could be reduced.

Bibliography and Further Reading

Cole, L. (1964), *Psychology of Adolescence*, Holt, Rinehart & Winston, New York.

Crane, A. R. (1956), *Journ. Educ. Res.*, 50, 227.

Duvall, E. M. (1962), *The Parent Teachers' Assn. Mag.*, 56, 10.

Finlay, S. E. (1967), Proc. Brit. Stud. Health Assn.

Flowerdew, G. (1965), *Lancet*, 2, 686.

Garrison, K. C. (1965), *The Psychology of Adolescence*, Prentice-Hall, New York.

Hunter, T. A. A. (1967), *Practitioner*, 198, 453.

Jephcott, P. (1967), *Time of One's Own*, Oliver & Boyd, Edinburgh and London.

Lehmann, I. J. (1962), *Journ. Educ. Psychol.*, 36, 1.

Miller, D. H. (1969), *The Age Between*, Cornmarket–Hutchinson, London.

Schofield, M. (1965), *The Sexual Behaviour of Young People*, Longman, London.

CHAPTER FOUR

Diseases and Health Problems of the Adolescent Student

THE STUDENTS are not a group who are particularly vulnerable to mortal disease. The causes of death are fortunately few and in order of frequency they are malignant disease (cancer of various organs and the leukaemias), accidents and suicide. The death rate for the age group of 15–25 is the lowest of any age group now that tuberculosis is virtually eradicated in the developed community. It is this relative freedom from mortality, therefore, that inevitably leads to the student community being considered, medically, as 'a healthy group'. From the point of view of morbidity, however, this is far from the truth, and physicians involved in the care of adolescents find that in terms of medical usage there is a consultation rate, per 1,000 students, of at least five attendances per year per student—a rate that compares in general family practice with that of the over 65s and the under 5s. There is a degree of supply and demand that prevails with the adolescent, however, which radically influences this rate, for the greater the number of physicians or counselling staff available for any set number of students, then the greater the number of students that avail themselves of the opportunity to consult. The reason for this is that much of the morbidity in the student population is minor illness, that is self-curing in three to four days, and if by lack of facilities they are unable to obtain ready advice, then they will, with time, not need it. Since, however, this is a learning group at a receptive age, correct advice may be helpful in putting into perspective the minor illness to which they, their eventual wives, children and families will always be prone. Moreover, there is a precise characteristic to illness, however minor, in the student community, one that must be well understood by all who have any dealings with them: and that is that it interferes with academic work. A van boy delivering bread can cope with his employment—albeit in discomfort—with a heavy cold and some degree of sinusitis perhaps, but a student in the same predicament cannot spend his customary two hours in the library, feels unwell and wants to go to bed, not being able to concentrate on writing up his thesis or seminar notes. A 'snowball phenomenon' then occurs where anxiety over not completing the academic programme is inevitably produced, and frustration with the effects of the minor illness grows out of all proportion to its real severity. The worry of this situation leads to a gradual exaggeration of concern with the feeling that 'something must be done'. Frustration, anxiety over falling behind in work (in a highly competitive situation) and discomfort combine to make even the heavy head 'cold' a more serious intrusion into every-day life than it is for many –academic concentration and physical fitness can be surprisingly closely related. The appreciation of this is an important part of their medical or nursing care—as important as teaching them that common illnesses cannot be immediately cured and must be coped with in a sensible symtomatic manner. The medical profession has, too, a duty to teach and impart its knowledge, and the fulfilment of this role is nowhere greater than when the patient is an intelligent, interested and questioning adolescent.

A succinct analysis of the organic-psychological illness pattern amongst students has been made by one experienced physician. One in every ten consultations in an academic community are for psychological reasons, one in every hundred require the further help of skilled psychiatrists, whilst one in a thousand students are overtly psychotic. In other words, 90 per cent of the consultations are for organic disease or disorder, albeit that each one, because of the special situation of the student, may have psychological overtones. In this chapter the organic disorders of the student will be considered; the psychological disorders merit separate discussion.

It will be recalled that earlier the observation was made that the adolescent is preoccupied with the development of his or her own body. Concern about whether whatever they find is 'normal' marks their consultation, and if it is not 'normal', then, rightly, they want to know why not. Thus many of their attendances for medical advice are initiated by changes in the physique. With regard to disease, they are vulnerable obviously to the common infectious diseases, and particularly because they live in a captive, often overcrowded community, prone to epidemic contagion. A list of the diseases to which a student is prone is not worth reciting here–they are no more and no less immune then the population as a whole. But there are specific areas of student health which have a particular significance.

To the present-day student hair 'fashions' are as basic to their social setting as ribbons of rank are to the world of the military. It may be surprising to some to note that, in the author's experience at least, the long hair of the student is often exceptionally clean. Perhaps in the community at large, where the 'drop-out' sleeps 'rough' and has little opportunity to pay attention to hygiene, this may not be the general case–and certainly it must be admitted (and will be discussed below) that the student community has its proportion of scabies, lice and parasitic infestation, nevertheless in general the 'privileged' adolescent is a 'clean' one. However, hair disorders are a source of anxiety to the student, and consultations about dandruff, what it is, how it should be treated, and how it can be avoided, are commonplace. Complaints of a receding hair-line on the forehead, of hair 'falling-out' and early baldness are also common, and they must be seen in the context of the youth who wants fundamentally to be reassured he is normal. True disease is rare, alopecia areata is most uncommon and generally where somewhat premature thinness of the hair or balding is seen in the male, there is a family history of this and son is just 'following in father's footsteps'. The fashion for wigs or hairpieces for girls does, however, tend to lead to less scrupulous hair hygiene; instead of having a 'hair-do' for a party she covers it up with a wig–but in view of their expense the female student population cannot follow this fashion as much as they might like to. There is an interesting observation to make, nevertheless, about fashion, and it is that long, free-flowing hair for girls has increased in popularity in proportion to so-called permissiveness–formality in social behaviour has passed as has the formal and precise hairstyle. This is not an individual hall-mark, just a general trend and the observation was made to the author by an experienced psychiatrist. The male too, of course, frequently shows both his independence from the parental fashion of 'a short back and sides' and his conformity to current adolescent fashion by growing the hair exceedingly long. But nevertheless, in the final year of academic studies, many of these styles vanish as the date of the interview with the prospective employer looms near–and there is a degree of sadness at times about witnessing this transformation from the freedom of youth to the conformity of adulthood.

Less important socially but more important to his future is the student's eyesight. Visual defects are common. It might be seen as an occupational hazard of many hours spent reading, writing and poring over books in, at times, bad light, but then also at this age the skull and orbit proportions are changing and the correction of even temporary visual defects is most important. Infections such as blepharitis are no more common than for other age groups, but allergies–often due to the gum of false eye-lashes–and accidents in the laboratory involving acid splashes, foreign bodies or explosions are more so. (Every accident in a university environment merits the most scrupulous attention, for frequently it is only by the follow-up

D

of the Occupational Health Staff or the Safety Officer that the careless procedures or methods of practice that have led to the accident are uncovered; and future ones must be prevented.) In view of the importance of visual correction, for someone who spends their waking hours almost totally involved in reading, note-taking or writing, most University or College Health Services have need of the part-time services of an experienced optician – and any student who wears spectacles should have an optician's assessment at least every eighteen months to two years.

Dental defects, too, are notoriously frequent. Children receive reasonable dental attention by virtue of their parents' interest; the student will commonly let his or her teeth rot until they ache. Fears of being hurt overtake the desire of the young man to conserve his teeth, but with the girls, at least, cosmetic motivation does lead to a generally better standard of dental care. Injury at sport – and many a football field becomes littered with upper and lower incisors – often leads to the dental chair, whilst the problems of the erupting 'wisdom' teeth secure the same attention. The addition of a dental surgeon to the staff of a University's Health Service becomes an inevitable necessity probably as soon as the population 'at risk' approaches the 2,000 number.

Specific Disorders of the Male

Genitally, because of the differing individual, social and ethnic rates of development, the male student under the care of any university physician will be at all stages of maturity. The majority will have completed their sexual growth, reached full adult testicular volume stage and penile length and be showing mature distribution of pubic and axillary hair, but some 20 per cent will be underdeveloped in the sense of not having completed yet this pattern of growth. Some will show disorders suggestive of medical neglect in their earlier lives and present at the age of 18 with an undescended testicle (1·5 per 1,000). This is a most serious abnormality and requires urgent surgical

attention—if its descent can be produced by surgical intervention, well and good; if not, because of the very real dangers
of malignant change, orchidectomy is required. Malignant
growth of the testicular tumours (e.g. seminoma) is seen at
this age and it is a lethal condition, survival from which is
unlikely five years after diagnosis. The foreskin of the late
adolescent should be fully retractable—and in the unfortunates
in whom this is not possible, circumscision is necessary because
of the hazards of paraphimosis (trapping of the retracted
foreskin ring behind the glans) when sexual excitement or
experience occurs. Hygiene is, in general, poor, and boys do
not seem to be taught by parents or teachers that regular penis
washing is desirable—the accumulation of the secretions
(smegma) and retained urine droplets frequently leads to
minor skin infection of the glans and foreskin (balanitis).
Anxiety about development is frequently seen as a cause of
consultation, and in particular the greater prominence of the
sebaceous and hair follicles on the foreskin and scrotum leads
many boys to the doctor's surgery to ask if 'this is all right'.
There may be latent guilt about masturbation behind the seeking
of reassurance, but many doctors have had shamefaced lads
in to see them about these hair follicles. Sexual excitement—
unrelieved by ejaculation—causes the classical pain in the
testicles known colloquially as 'lover's nuts' and presents
therefore a difficult problem when advice is requested. Does
one advise the boy to deliberately 'go further' or 'to stop'?
Often it is enough to explain to the boy why he gets this pain
of congestion and muscular ischaemia due to continual spasm
and leave it to him to decide how to avoid it. Anxiety about
failure of erections for the experienced, or about problem-
associated with masturbation for others, are frequent complaints. The explanations that worry, desire to 'perform well',
thinking about examinations and fear of pregnancy occurring
are normal sexual suppressants and a comparison with
'businessman's impotence' are gratefully accepted. Where else
can a boy with such problems get information? Books? The

majority are grossly unreliable. Instruction in classes? There is none, and yet a good case could be made for the need to add to all educational curricula the subjects of sexual hygiene and technique. It is after all a normal function of the body. With regard to masturbation, it is now surely obvious that it is not the practice that is harmful but the guilt and anxiety, that tradition has too frequently instilled into everyone, that follows its occurrence. Natural *post coitam tristam* has been made of use by the preachers of the past, to create an unnatural guilt. Many a young student has felt inconsolable isolation and guilt about the evidence on his pyjamas of a perfectly healthy nocturnal emission—and it is ironic that society should frustrate their capabilities of procreation, produce this inevitable effect and then render the individual a subject of guilty anxiety. Bizarre consequences can occur and the author recently had to refer, as an emergency, an otherwise normal student to the surgeons for suturing his penis because he had tried to saw it off with a razor blade. No drugs were involved and psychiatrically there was no psychosis—he was just exceptionally guilty. The great majority of male adolescents masturbate—it is strange if they do not—until they form a stable sexual relationship where mutual relief takes over from the lonely seeking of comfort. It is a physiological occurrence for which society in the past has written strange rules which, without exception, were misguided.

Specific Disorders of the Female

The adolescent breast is a developing organ. It undergoes cyclical changes, with premenstrual tenderness and post menstrual slackness, and during late adolescence is generally increasing in size (1 in. to 2 in. bust measurement increase from 18–20 years). Too large and the girl feels worried, too small and she worries too. It is not exactly a symbol of status amongst students, but both hypertrophy and lack of development lead to consultations. Treatment, apart from reassurance, is quite wrong unless the disparity from normal is gross and hormonal interference with the slowly developing girl can provoke unlimited upsets of her physiology. The excessive breasts often accompany an excessively well-covered body, and a reducing diet with proper exercise can do much to normalise the physique and restore the girl to social confidence. Cysts and adenomas are relatively common and require surgical attention – it is exceedingly rare to find a malignancy, but every abnormality should nevertheless receive skilled attention.

Ovarian abnormalities occur probably at the same rate of incidence as do testicular ones in the males (1·5 per 1,000). Cysts and other secretory-tissue disturbances will show either by a hormonal reflection of their presence in an altered menstrual pattern or by severe dysmenorrhoea as they become congested. The diagnosis is not easy, particularly if the girl is 'virgo intacta', and often it is only confirmed by an examination under anaesthesia performed by the gynaecologist. When found, they are rarely malignant and invariably the simple resection that is necessary leaves the girl's future fertility unimpaired. Sometimes when a laparotomy is performed for a possible diagnosis of appendicitis it is only then that the true cause of the pain – an ovarian cyst – is seen and dealt with, the 'normal' appendix being removed prophylactically. 'Mittelschmerz' is common – the pain of ovulation, which occurs usually in the second post-menstrual week, and which may be accompanied by a slight vaginal 'spotting' of blood-stained discharge. The ovary on one or other side will be tender to deep palpation, and if it is the one on the right then the girl is often labelled as a 'grumbling appendix' – wrongly.

Menstruation can be scanty or profuse, regular or chaotic, agony or hardly noticeable, absent for many months or delayed by travel, anxiety or the newly implanted foetus – there is an enormous all-embracing menstrual spectrum, and the girl who can always predict her cyclical calendar accurately is lucky, somewhat uncommon and liable at any time to join the others who cannot. In the absence of genital pathology, severe and debilitating dysmenorrhoea is a genuine psychological symptom. Not because she imagines it, but because she has either been 'trained' to expect it or because she has other anxieties that aggravate the normal pain of spasmodic ischaemia, or because her mother always had it! The incidence of consultations about dysmenorrhoea rises dramatically in the summer– impending examination time–because the girl who could put up with pain normally and cope with self-medication is worried about it interfering with her examination revision. The cyclical hormonal control methods now available–such as the 'pill'–have revolutionised its treatment and the 'waiting lists' for 'D and C's' (dilatation and curettage) by the gynae-cologists have dramatically fallen. Irregular menstruation in whatever form is a great nuisance for the girl–excessive losses initiate or aggravate anaemia, scanty losses make her feel she is not a 'whole woman'. The regulation of these problems, or the demonstration by short-term therapy that regulation is always possible, is part of everyday adolescent gynaecology.

Vaginal discharges, like menstruation, can vary with a rain-bow-like character. From the normal opalescent secretions that most girls experience, particularly pre-menstrually, to thick yellowish and offensive curdy deposits causing extreme discomfort and irritation, the whole range is seen. Guilt and worry play their part as girls fear that the manual stimulation they have permitted–against their 'better' or traditional judgement and yet as a result of their natural affection and desires–have produced a venereal disease. Bizarre reactions may occur and girls may soak their genitalia in neat disinfectant, causing the most severe sensitivity reactions–just as excessive abandon with deodorants may do the same. A proper gynae-cological examination is always necessary and swabbing bacteriologically, answers many queries. The most offensive discharge is caused by the not infrequent neglect to remove a tampon, and no amount of cream or pessaries will cure that, until it is extracted. Retained tampons are also a source of a very embarrassed 'emergency' call by young girls, and whenever

one arrives at the girl's address and she admits that even her
boy-friend 'could not get it out', one can assume that its
'disappearance' was associated with her boy-friend's activities
in any case. The common infective organisms are monilial,
which with the trichomonads, account for the vast majority
of cases – the gonococcus is rare, but may, nevertheless, be
lurking. Hence the value of a 'routine' investigation.

Vulval warts are seen rarely, but they occur from time to
time and wherever they do – as with the trichomonas infections and other venereal diseases – both 'partners' must be
treated. Infections of the Bartholin glands between the labia
may be acute sources of pain and discomfort, and often the
girl tends to complain of dyspareunia (painful intercourse)
as her symptom of this infection. Very troublesome abscess
formation may require their surgical marsupialisation –
otherwise they respond quite readily to antibiotic therapy.

Dyspareunia, as a complaint in a young unmarried woman,
has been known to cause righteous indignation amongst
some physicians unused to the current social behaviour
patterns, but it is a genuine and often very significant complaint. Pain during intercourse or at penetration may be
simply gynaecological – infections of the mucusa, bartho-
linitis, or due to endometrial deposits in the retro-vaginal
peritoneal pouch, each requiring the appropriate therapy – but
it can also be a symptom of genuine disaffection with sexual
activity. Muscular spasm, painful and inexperienced thrusting
by the male and the total lack of any orgasmic sensations are
not uncommonly found as the burden of the intense and
would-be permissive girl. Sexual athleticism may be tried out,
not for enjoyment but because they have read about it; and
when the anxious, worried girl is trying her best to get something out of the experience and constantly failing, it is not
surprising that she complains – but unfortunately she will
attend the surgery unhappily convinced that it is her own
inadequacy at fault. Love is not a gymnastic performance. In
youth there are many ways of learning, and it is sometimes the

doctor who has to explain what relaxation, patience and mutual physical respect are—with regard to orgasms there is no 'technique' and they are happy to learn primarily that they are normal now, and that life still holds some pleasure for them in the future.

Localised irritation of the vulva is common and the pruritis (itching) that accompanies it may be a source of considerable embarrassment and distress. If discharge is responsible, then therapy offers a good response, but the occasional diabetic may present with monilial vulvitis as the first symptom and appropriate checking is necessary. In some cases, however, it is a true neurodermatitis, initiated by a variety of psychological reasons, and considerable discussion is necessary at times to try and gain the sufferer insight—psychotherapeutic agents may well produce a better response than local and topical agents. The obsessional use of deodorants—especially the topically overwhelming spray—is not without the hazard of sensitivity, which may also show itself by the complaint of pruritis vulvae.

The female urethra is shorter than the male's (by 3 in.), lies within the muscular upper wall of the vagina, and its aperture is covered by the labia minora—as such these facts may well be responsible for the greater incidence of urinary infections in the female than in the male. Cystitis is a burden of womanhood, and 'honeymoon' cystitis is the price many a a girl pays for having her vaginal wall traumatised during sexual intercourse. Frequency of passing urine and a 'burning' feeling are the hall-marks of 'honeymoon' cystitis and it is not a difficult epidemiological problem to unravel why the majority of doctors see it as a complaint in their Monday morning clinics. Whatever the disputed pathology, urinary infections are common in young adolescent girls and occasionally persist or develop into renal infections. Bacteriuria, if demonstrably present, is serious and requires vigorous treatment; every urinary complaint should be bacteriologically investigated and treated appropriately, with a follow-up 'test of cure'. It is in this policy that lies the hope of preventing chronic pyelonephritis, hypertension and a reduced life expectancy.

Generalised Disorders and Infections in Adolescence

There are no specific diseases of adolescence but the 'privileged' ones pay a certain small price for being students–they have to live together in one large community, be it hall of residence, college, multi-occupied house or shared flat. They eat together in large numbers and live generally in close proximity physically, as human beings who go from crowded lecture to lunch-time refectory queue; hence they are more exposed to epidemic contagion than are most other members of the public– a feature they share with inmates of any institution. Food-poisoning in a college can be a disaster, influenza can immobilise the majority of the community all at once, and waves of a virus epidemic can flow back and forth affecting far larger numbers at one time than one might ever find in the normal population. Proximity lends itself to contagious disease.

All the usual range of infection is seen in students–upper respiratory infection, sore throats, mumps, measles, rubella and chicken-pox, virus infections giving epidemics of diarrhoea and vomiting, hepatitis, and occasionally tuberculosis. Rareities like brucellosis, anthrax, tetanus and rheumatic fever occur occasionally, but in general it is the 'common diseases that are common'.

Glandular fever, or infectious mononucleosis, is probably the one disease that physicians involved in the care of adolescents see more of than any other doctor. An unidentified virus is responsible; it is a debilitating acute-on-chronic disease often lasting from three to six weeks with the sequelae of a predisposition to fatigue and other infections and is a serious threat to the student in loss of academic time. No one can afford nearly a term off their studies and be unaffected academically. Its transmission is probably by contact, although to call it the 'kissing disease' is nonsense; surprisingly, however, there will often be three or four students sharing a flat, one who gets glandular fever and the other three are spared. Its contact transmission therefore is not great. There is no effective treatment (steroids abort its acute stage) other than symptomatic, and no preventitive means are yet available. The interesting idea has been put forward, however, that the virus responsible may either cause leukaemia or glandular fever, and an attack of glandular fever confers immunity against its far more sinister colleague.

Anaemia affects 20 per cent of all women in the developed countries, and it is certainly common as an iron-deficiency sign in young girls. Not just menstrual losses but also dietary deficiencies are responsible. A self-catering student is not given to frequent indulgence in rare steaks, kidney and liver dishes and lacks the adeptness or the financial means to ensure a good balanced diet. The male does not escape anaemia either, and it is a frequent finding of the Blood Transfusion Service that up to 5 per cent of would-be young donors have to be rejected because their need is greater than the service's. The provision of adequate access to laboratory diagnostic facilities is therefore a *sine qua non* of any large College Health Service.

Obesity is common – the 'beer-belly' of the games player is not always solid muscle, and the girl who suddenly finds she needs to go to the 'outsize' department will find herself very quickly in her physician's consulting room. Carbohydrate is cheap, chip potatoes are a satisfying 'gastric blotter' for the stomach full of beer, and the adolescent has a normal voracious appetite that cannot be satisfied by the delicacies of crêpes flambées or a hollandaise sauce – even if he or she could afford them. This is, therefore, an important age to establish weight consciousness. The habits of late adolescence may well last over to later life, and a stone overweight is statistically as hazardous to life expectancy as it is to smoke twenty-five cigarettes a day. Slimming for the youth should be achieved by dietary direction, not by medication – the savoury palate is a healthier acquisition than a dependence on an appetite suppressant. Moreover, there is a great need for energy—slimming is not to be achieved by starvation unless at the cost of headaches, dizziness, fatigue and faintness.

Alcoholism is rare as a chronic disorder of adolescence, but in the acute form it has probably occurred to most people at some time and certainly many students learn only how to 'take their liquor' at the cost of a night's vomiting in a hedge or else on their knees before the lavatory, praying for death to intervene and grant relief. The hazard of acute alcoholic coma and inhaling vomit is a serious one, but fortunately rare; provided the sufferer can 'sleep it off' under supervision there are no long-term effects. The commonest cause of adolescent drunkenness is the party where drinks are unwisely mixed or the mixture that is served as a 'witches brew' of everything including absolute alcohol from the chemistry department!

Lice, scabies, fleas and bed-bug bites are seen with increasing frequency by comparison to earlier years, but nevertheless they are not common. The problem has developed with the habit of sharing beds—the use of a friend's bed for a 'guest' at a week-end or the advent of the student fringe group on the scene. This group is increasing, the 'drop-outs' who circulate from college to college, who sleep rough in the summer and 'cadge' any accommodation they can in the winter—girls with all they possess in a paper-carrier bag and boys who shoulder the ex-army ruck-sac that contains but one shirt, perhaps a comb, and a guitar and radio. Given the chance of finding a college bedroom they will take it, and leave their parasites for the unsuspecting owner; or else a girl will pass them on as part of the price of a few minutes' pleasure.

Venereal disease is also increasing, but again in the student population it is comparatively rare. The student population in general keeps its copulation 'in the family', and the spread of VD is isolated to groups of whom one is in contact with a girl in the town, or who met a 'fascinating' continental waiter during the holidays. Syphilis is confined (in the author's experience at any rate) to homosexual males who prostitute themselves in the larger cities, and they provide the greatest danger to the homosexual student. Gonorrhoea very rapidly announces its presence to the male and invariably receives prompt medical attention; the history of 'contact', however, must be followed up, and where it is a girl student she readily co-operates in treatment, having been shocked and surprised to find she is infected. Non-specific urethritis is also seen with moderate frequency in male students but clears rapidly with treatment. The one remarkable feature about VD in students is their ignorance of what it is, how you get it, and what the symptoms are. In a survey, designed as a questionnaire about symptomatology and completed by 200 females students, only 1 per cent scored correct answers. Both the girls who answered correctly had had VD before! The rest thought that symptoms from 'frigidity' to 'loss of pubic hair' were appropriate. Once again, unless learnt in the bitter school of experience, where else does our adolescent gain his or her knowledge about venereal disease? There is little if any school instruction, no pattern of widespread health education, and thus ignorance indubitably contributes to the spread of venereal disease.

Of course for most adolescents the most outwardly obvious and inwardly hurtful of diseases are those of the skin. After upper respiratory infections they are the most frequent cause of consultation – the 'teenage spots' are almost a hall-mark of adolescence. Acne is of unknown aetiology. A disorder of the sebaceous glands, probably brought about by imbalance between the secondary sexual hormones and the growth hormone, it is characterised by overactive glands, blockage of the pores with comedone (blackhead) formation and secondary infection with the normal skin bacteria. The face, shoulders and chest are affected, often in a descending order as age advances, and degrees of dermatological disability are seen from the pimples on the forehead to the permanently disfiguring cystic abscesses that leave life-long scars. The treatment involves attempts to reduce skin bacteria, suppress infection, minimise the sebaceous and fatty secretions and to obtain remissions of exacerbations. It cannot be cured, it has little to do with diet, sexual activity or eating cocoa, and it is surrounded with myths and commercial cosmetic enterprise. Sunshine (or artificial UVL), detergent soaps and antibiotics orally or topically are beneficial, and experienced medical attention can do much to relieve the adolescents' acneiform burden. The burden is not all shown on the face, however, because if the student feels he is 'spotty' and repulsive, then it can be a severely socially inhibiting disorder. The dance, the date and the party can be viewed with distress when the invitee has a blind-boil-laden cheek, and the young lad is rarely anxious to take off his shirt in public (and get the sunlight that would be beneficial) when his shoulders are pock-marked and pustular. There is a menstrual cyclic aggravation and also good evidence that shows there is a rise in sebaceous gland activity with anxiety and stress. Thus the disorder of acne has psychological and physiological ramifications often quite disproportionate to the actual degree of skin sepsis, and the sufferer needs sympathetic handling, enthusiastic treatment and constant interest by the doctor – 'you'll grow out of it' is not good enough.

Psoriasis and eczema show exacerbations together with the increased stress that a student inevitably experiences from time to time. The 'rise and fall of the leaf' precipitates a flare up of atopic eczema, as much as does the advent of the final examinations. Neurodermatitis is not as common as it is in the more mature age groups of the population, but warts – plantar and on the hand – are as frequently seen as they are in children. Diathermic destruction and various acidic, caustic or low-temperature topical applications are the standard forms of treatment which meet with varying success. Skin sepsis, as boils, paranychia or axillary abscesses are seen with the same incidence as they are in the normal population, as is severe sunburn and chilblains, but a major contrast exists in the matter of fungal infections. With sexual maturity and adult apocrine and mepocrine sweat gland secretions in the axillae and groin the pH of the skin in these regions is altered and rendered fungus-prone. The fungi of tinea cruris and pedis are rife in the student community, spread by such medieval horrors as the rugby club mutual bath, inadequately disinfected ablution facilities and the habit of the male student of washing his socks, underpants and athletic support in the same wash-bowl! The rash of the male groin with a scrotal itch and its spread to the upper inner thigh is common – and the peeling interdigital skin of the toes of both sexes even more so. Adequate fungicidal preparations and instructions on hygiene with the advice to buy more socks than the two pairs usually possessed are therapeutically effective. Ringworm is not unusual, and often a history of the landlady's 'mangy' cat or the family's geriatric dog is forthcoming on enquiry.

Occasionally one sees, as the soul of the body is reflected on the face, a degree of self-excoriation in the often thin, intro-verted girl. She picks her spots with ferocious and persistent enthusiasm. For her, psychotherapeutic agents are often more effective than topical preparations, but she serves for the doctor as the constant reminder that in the young adult it is less the illness and more the cause or the psychological effects of the disorder that are of overwhelming importance. For no one is it more appropriate than for the privileged adolescent that there is a *mens sane in corpore sano*.

CHAPTER FIVE

Anxiety and Stress

YOUTH is a struggle. Torn between social desires to conform and yet to be original, pressed by the physical demands of a maturing soma on an immature psyche, and stressed further by the competition of an academic life should in the case of students – it is hardly surprising that there should be psychological casualties amongst those who find themselves privileged by further education. The office boy and the shop girl have problems enough with their parental relationships, sexual maturation, struggle for economic independence and role identification, but the student will undergo all these and more. It might be thought to be a small price to pay for the rewards in later life that academic success might bring in terms of career and earnings. There is some reason in this argument, if only from the view that should they survive and succeed then they have proved themselves in the intellectual and personality initiation rites that contemporary society has created for them. Someone who can 'take on the chin', as it were, all the stresses of being a student, is someone who will cope with all the stressful demands of a managerial and administrative career in later life without breakdown. Nevertheless, there is one point of supreme importance often missed by those who argue that the student's life should be governed by the jungle law of survival of the fittest – and that is the point of waste. Contemporary society cannot afford to waste any of its intellectual élite, not only because there is not enough of it, but also because it is too expensive to do so. A student in the UK for example, costs, in terms of capital investment, fees, maintenance and tuition, some £2,000 a year, and if anyone should fail for reasons that might have been averted, then that failure represents a considerable and tragic loss to the economy. This is looking at it broadly – the cost of failure to the individual, the family and to the future mental health of the student concerned is not measurable in monetary values but may be enormous in terms of immediate frustration, the long-term unrealised potential and the permanent scarring of confidence or initiative. Thus anything that can be done to support the individual through the psychological crises of his or her development period, or that can be done to identify whatever it is that might be the most harmful aspect of any academic institution, or its organisation, is worthy.

The stresses of a university or college life are considerable and complex, and there are four main and easily recognisable aetiological factors that contribute to aggravating the normal developmental problems faced by any student. They are problems of adaption, family difficulties, sexual conflicts, and the feeling of being a lonely or isolated member of a large institution.

Firstly, there is the diffcult adaptation necessary for transition from school to university. This is very variable in its effects on the individual, according to the student's background and methods of teaching and learning at school. Some students arrive at university much better able to accept the larger degree of responsibility for organising themselves and their studies than others. In part, this reflects their academic experience whilst still at school. The greatest effort at adaptation, of course, has to be made by students from a different cultural background; nevertheless, each and every one has for the first time to organise their own lives. From washing socks to making their allowances last and coping with a timetable that demands a consistent output of academic work, that is probably unsupervised until after it is produced –

the new student has to be totally self-sufficient from arrival at college. Moreover, the 'bright' individual from a small school, used to being academically advanced, suddenly finds that his or her contemporaries are equally or even better endowed intellectually and is faced therefore with the necessity of adjustment, for the first time perhaps, to this humbling fact of life.

Secondly come problems stemming from family difficulties and pressures. It is frequently obvious that a student's difficulties are related to conflict that arises from the family's reaction to his or her stage of development. Parents who for their own reasons cannot 'let go' or, on the other hand, parents who lose touch too soon, and parents who are divided, ill or living out an imaginary and personal role of academic distinction through their children, all make the student's life more difficult. The student may re-enact therefore at university the conflict between dependency and rebellion that he has adopted at home, or worse, find himself at college simply because it was his parents who wanted him to go, and the only motivation that is present for following an academic life is parental gratification. At this age, too, some 15 per cent of adolescents will come from homes 'broken' by death of either parent, divorce or separation, and the relationship that the student has with the surviving parent will not necessarily be a normal one—for they are torn by the situation they find themselves in of relative independence as a student, with feelings of exaggerated responsibility towards their deserted or deprived parent.

Thirdly, there are sexual conflicts, often brought to the fore by the new freedoms of the academic environment. These cause a good deal of anxiety at all levels in the university. Among students, previously accepted moral standards may be questioned, as are all other attitudes to life, and relationships entered into by immature individuals can lead to upsetting consequences—particularly if gratifications of dependent needs or rebellion against parental opposition to the relationships

E

figure too prominently as motives. It is possible that a degree of apparently deliberate failure to use contraceptives where they are available, and the consequent unwanted pregnancy, more often results from the unconscious acting out of problems of this kind than from mere carelessness. Similarly, with the earlier physical maturation that has occurred in the present generations, the greater degree of leisure and the contemporary sense of sexual values that the present society has adopted, emotional relationships are entered into but to students are denied their fruition in marriage and children – though not to their less academically endowed colleagues who left school earlier – and there is a considerable degree of frustration in this fact of student life.

Fourthly, as academic institutions increase in size there is a growing gulf in communication at all levels. Tutors may be so only in name, lecturers may address a sea of unknown faces, and professors may only know personally those students who have got into difficulties with examinations or the authorities. In the large technical colleges the 'sandwich' course may often mitigate against personal supervision of a student's full-time academic career, whilst in the large faculties of a university there may be as many as 200 students taking a first-year course in any one subject, the teaching of which is sometimes delegated to junior academic staff because the senior staff are more closely involved with the post-graduates and research. Staff-student committees, and student participation in university government have been among the more rational demands of the vociferous protestors in recent years and they represent a very reasonable move to finding a solution to the problem of anonymity in the academic machine – that is one felt particularly by the student.

The problems of stress in the academic community, therefore are complex, and they evolve basically into those of identifying the vulnerable, recognising the causes and mitigating the effects; and a considerable amount of research has been devoted to the best ways of doing all three. The first difficulty that arises, however, in trying to compare the research done in many diverse institutions is that of nomenclature.

Quite apart from the many diverse and often conflicting views on the aetiology of states of psychological disturbance, there is little uniformity in the methods of describing and labelling such states, or indeed in the degree to which they are recognised. Thus, what one college physician calls 'examination nerves', another may refer to as 'nervous breakdown', and a third as 'personality defect'. Moreover, whenever anyone takes a particular interest in psychological illness amongst students, then the incidence will inevitably rise, since its recognition rate will rise and the apportionment of the statistics is perhaps distorted. One may take what may seem as a simple example dysmenorrhoea, or painful menstruation. The prevalance of this complaint in the young and unmarried female population is high, but the incidence of consultation for medical help in the student population rises every summer term to be almost twice that seen during the previous two terms. There is no readily acceptable reason for this seasonal rise apart from the fact that most university examinations occur in the summer and so it would be simple to suggest that many of the cases seen are psychological. An organically orientated physician may claim that it is all due to cervical spasm and uterine ischaemia, and that the girls wait a couple of terms before plucking up enough courage to complain—the psychologically interested would assert in all probability that the anxiety over examinations exaggerates the pain and it is not dysmenorrhoea they are consulting about but one symptom of their stress. Which is it? Probably somewhere between the two, with the stress of the exam rendering intolerable what previously they could cope with themselves—but the main point is that the classification of their consultation will depend on the physician's interpretation and interest.

Nevertheless, there are acceptable averages, and trends that are identifiable, between one institution and another. It is a reasonable simplification of the UK statistics to assert that one in ten consultations in student health care is for psychological reasons, one in a hundred referral for psychiatric advice, and one in a thousand prove to be psychotic. A comparable synthesis has been made at Harvard for the American student, where it is reported that: 'Recent statistics from college health services indicate that for every 10,000 students, 1,000 will have emotional conflicts of sufficient severity to warrant professional help; 300 to 400 will have feelings of depression severe enough to impair their efficiency; 100 to 200 will be apathetic and unable to organise their efforts . . . and 15 to 25 will become ill enough to require hospitalisation.' In more detail, however, there are many general findings of particular importance.

Firstly, it is found that university life is more stressful for women than it is for men – in terms of consultation for psychological illness. A five-year cohort study of students at two universities was undertaken in 1961, and the rates for psychological disorder among women were significantly higher than the rates for men. In one the prevalance was 9·0 per cent for men and 14·6 per cent for women during the first year at university, and in the other it was 9·1 per cent for men and 13·5 per cent for women. At another university, Still found that the annual pattern of consultation in 1966 agreed with the trends of these earlier findings, and Edmond confirmed the same statistically significant difference between the sexes at a university and the Institute of Science and Technology. In the United States there is a considerable variation in the recording rates for psychological illness amongst students (e.g. at Yale 10 per cent seek what is termed 'psychiatric help', at Harvard 8 per cent, at Kansas 4 per cent and an investigation carried out by the National Institute of Mental Health in several colleges in the Washington area has evidence that 12 per cent show signs of psychiatric disturbance, whereas 30 per cent suffer from minor psychological troubles); nevertheless, the pattern of greater vulnerability amongst the females is maintained.

It is a matter perhaps for conjecture as to why this is so. There have been, unfortunately, few adequate surveys of the non-academic population for comparison, but those that have been reported do, however, show a degree of similarity over this one feature of psychological illness in this age group of the late adolescent—i.e. the prominence of the female sufferer. In one survey, for example, of forty-six family practices, rates of 1·9 per annum per thousand at risk (age group 15–24 years) were found for males and 3·0 for females of the same age group. A finding which matches in sex-difference the pattern amongst student populations and one which also reflects perhaps what might be considered as the much greater vulnerability of the student to psychological disorder than other members of the same age group in the population. Care must be taken, however, not to extrapolate too much from surveys done in general practice, for the influence on the student of having a personalised health service available for their psychological problems is considerable in its effect on the statistics by permitting their ready reporting. Moreover, since any psychological upset grossly distorts academic work capacity, the student will seek help where the shop girl will carry on, albeit perhaps short-tempered and discourteous to the customer! The predominance of the female in the statistics has led some writers to identify risk with femininity—and assert, not without some evidence, that the more 'female' the girl the more likely she is to have poor academic motivation and eventually to withdraw (her ideals perhaps being those of marriage, children and a home). The academically dedicated girl may well have been, therefore, a self-selected feature of the earlier generations.

Secondly (and this is elaborated elsewhere), the overseas student is more prone than the indigent to psychological upset and stress. The problems of a foreign cultural environment, greater stress due to the expectations of those 'at home' in their own country, and the difficulties of study when trained by different techniques, are common experiences for the overseas student, to say nothing of language and expression in examination difficulties.

Thirdly, however, there is some international consistency in the inter-faculty differences of consultation for psychological reasons that is borne out by a study of the statistics. The author would not go as far as Brautigam from Poland who claims that the higher prevalence of psychosis among theologians and psychologists is accounted for by the pre-pscyhotic personality of the individuals that makes them choose those subjects for study, but there is no doubt that certain characteristics which direct a student's choice towards studying certain subjects are shown up in the prevalence rates of psychological disturbance. It could be that, having exhausted his or her academic potential at school in the subjects studied there (say Modern Languages and History), a university entrant then decides to follow something 'new' (say Economics, Sociology, Psychology) with poor motivation for the subject other than a desire for a 'change', and then finds difficulties because of their intellectual inability to cope. Nevertheless, some explanation is needed as to why the Arts student and those from the faculties of Economics, Sociology, Law and Education, comprising perhaps 40 per cent of a university population, produce 60 per cent of the psychological reactions—a difference not accounted for statistically by the proportion of women. In Manchester the faculties of Arts and Economics led the field with rates of 24–28 per 1,000 over three years for the former and 38–39 per 1,000 for the latter when it came to an analysis of examination strain, whilst at Sheffield similar findings were reported by Stengel and Davies. At the University of Rome an enquiry into the incidence of psychological disturbance in relation to study difficulties provided similar results, with those who were in the department of Economic Sciences proving the most vulnerable. Why should this be so—with European statistics matched by those of the USA, where for example Farnsworth (Harvard) reports that the 'humanities' students suffer a consistently higher rate of psychological illness than the scientists? Weiss, Segal and Sokol of Dartmouth College, New Hampshire, have, from their research, some interesting light to throw on this problem. They studied emotional impairment among American male college students over a period of six years, by means of the Minnesota Multiphasic Personality Inventory—a questionnaire —which was used as part of routine selection procedures. Amongst their many findings (one main one was a rise of 2·5 times the impairment rate over the six years) was the correlation of a greater verbal ability with emotional impairment. The more explicit and expressive a student in his or her use of vocabulary the greater the tendency to emotional reaction. These students also had the highest drop-out rate (33 per cent). Thus the verbally able, the 'communicators', the literate and seusate who were able to express themselves, also showed in common with these abilities a higher incidence of emotional impairment—it may be far from cause and effect, but the characteristic of verbal ability is also that which must mitigate for a choice of an 'arts' subject. Scientific study tends to be disciplined, and although it offers a training in certain forms of criticism, the emotional, flamboyant and literate gravitate more towards the arts, where individual expression is welcomed and personal criticism rewarded. There are therefore some personality characteristics which in the young child produce a leaning to or away from scientific studies, and which in later life are reflected in the incidence of neurosis and psychological upset. Our means of detecting these characteristics are immature and unreliable, but the rates of breakdown that occur—in those who have self-selected their subject of study—speak for themselves. Why this is so cannot be answered with any certainty. It is interesting to note two other features, however, of this faculty difference—the 'protestors' tend also to come from the economic and sociology departments, and medicine internationally shows the lowest rates of all for psychological upset or neurotic disturbance. Perhaps the vocational aspect of the course of study taken up is reflected in the incidence rates, for engineers and dentists show the same low rates as medical students, and they are all students who know their career prospects and have high motivation for studying the subject. In contrast, the arts student has still to look for a job after graduation, and apart from his or her personal developmental problems they face problems of the future employment and career choice, which must be resolved at the same time as competing academically. There is much room for speculation about the cause, and research into effect, and it may be that more precise information of aetiology will lead to useful selection techniques, perhaps course modifications and a greater degree of vocational training in every academic subject. The preventive aspect otherwise is denied much hope of success, and college authorities and university physicians are destined to continue to just 'pick up the pieces'.

Fourthly, and it is a familiar fact to everyone involved with student health affairs, psychological disturbance in this age group shows a predominantly somatic symptomatology where the patients are more likely to complain of a physical disturbance than to admit to being anxious. Insomia is common, and if it is a complaint that the student cannot 'get off to sleep', then it is transparently due to anxiety and worry combined often with having worked late. Insight into the origins of this disturbance is denied to few, and this type of late evening insomnia requires little more than the prescription of some anxiolytic or mild hypnotic (a pint or two of beer or cocoa and a warm bath may often be enough) to overcome the problem which can be seen as an occupational hazard of any intellectual activity. Other symptoms of stress and anxiety, however, may be more disguised and may take their colouring from the local environment and the student's background. There is a degree of narcissism about adolescence, and the anxious student will frequently complain about the body they are endowed with – 'I am not as fit as I was' is the neurosis of the athletic type, whilst 'I cannot concentrate' is the complaint of the previously obsessional academic worker. Concern about physical development, whether it be irregular menstruation or worry about the prominence of hair follicles on the scrotum, may mask an underlying anxiety about apparent failure to succeed in academic competition. Many have, understandably enough, not yet come to terms with themselves in deciding what part sexual activity should play in their lives at this stage in their careers and have difficulties with the priorities. These will present with a variety of gynaecological or psychological complaints—from the boy who complains of impotence, when in fact he is anxious and guilty about the way he is 'using' a girl for physical gratification and does not love her, to the girl who complains about breast tenderness, nausea and putting on weight because of the oral contraceptive, when in fact her dissatisfaction is due to her frustrated maternal urge and the instability of her relationship with a boy who will not remain strictly with her. A student's anxiety, of a degree sufficient to impair work seriously, may express itself in exaggerated concern for a member of his family—worrying about father's health may be entirely genuine or quite distorted and form an excuse for failing to meet academic standards or, frequently where there is a family history, developing a neurosis about the same disease. Thus we see the cardiac neurosis of the son, where the father has had a coronary thrombosis, or the girl constantly finding normal lumps of breast tissue in the secretory phase where the mother has had a mastectomy.

Finally, and perhaps surprisingly, examinations *per se* are not the main cause of anxiety in the academic community. In the great majority (79 per cent) where there are so-called 'examination nerves', there is a history of neurotic or anxiety type reactions to other stresses in life apart from examinations. Severe reactions occur more frequently when the stress of the examination is added to some previously existing psychological disturbance. The well-adjusted cope with the examination stress in the same way that they coped with developmental, family, personal and sexual problems. There is little evidence that shows the examination system to be causative of breakdown. Examination anxiety, when severe, is usually demonstrably related to personal conflict and hardly ever bears much relationship to academic potential. Poor motivation to graduate, a desire perhaps not to leave the freedom of the academic community, failure to accept the responsibility of undertaking a career, remorse at not having done any academic work for the previous year–these are the typical findings in the 'exam nerves' cases and not unexpectedly. In the student population one is in fact dealing with a group who have self-selected themselves for further academic training by demonstrating in earlier adolescence an ability to perform well in examinations. When they develop acute and severe 'examination nerves' it is not that they are incapable, or unable to do it, or that the examination system is unfair, but that they have failed in some way to adjust and adapt continually to the demands of maturing. The mild cases are normal and some degree of anxiousness about how they will perform is a natural conscience spurring them to greater efforts–the severe cases who withdraw from all work, and become apathetic in personality and attitude, are not normal personalities. They are depressed and their illness is much more severe and may be much more serious. Their illness then is usually the result of prolonged and chronic anxiety–anxiety over many features of their life and not just examinations. It was Hippocrates who recognised that prolonged anxiety became 'melancholy', and it is as if these patients have exhausted their innate ability to adjust. Stress and anxiety for some is a spur, a challenge and an excitement, or is part of life's pattern that they learn to adapt to, as they grow, mature and resolve their difficulties with help or by themselves–for others whose personalities are less strong or more handicapped, stress becomes corrosive, anxiety becomes chronic and depression intervenes.

Bibliography and Further Reading

Braceland, F. J., and Farnsworth, D. L. (1969), *Maryland Med. Journ.*, 18, (4), 67.

Brautigam, W. (1966), Communication at WHO Symposium on Student Health Services, Cracow.

Davies, C., and Stengel, E. (1966), Proc. Brit. Stud. Health Assn.

Edmonds, P. (1969), Paper presented at Res. and Study Group Meeting, Brit. Stud. Health Assn.

Erikson, E. (1956), Proc. of First Int. Conf. on Student Mental Health, Princeton, Riverside Press, Cambridge, USA.

Frighi, L. F. (1967), 'Psychological and Psychic Disturbances in Relation to Study Difficulties and Examination Strain', *Stud. Health News*, 3.

Gundle, S. (1968), 'Protection of Mental Health in Univ. of the USA', *Stud. Health News*, 5.

Henderson, A. S., *et al.* (1967), *Brit. med. J.*, **1,** 83.

Irwin, E. M. (1967), Proc. Brit. Stud. Health Assn.

Kidd, C. B. (1965), *Brit. J. prev. soc. Med.*, 19, 143.

—— (1966), Proc. Brit. Stud. Health Assn.

——, and Caldbeck Meenan, J. (1966), *Brit. J. Psych.*, **112,** 57.

Miller, D. H. (1967), *Med. World*, Jan. 7.

Ryle, A. (1967), *ibid*, 13.

—— (1970), G. P., Feb. 27, 4.

Still, R. J. (1967), 'The Mental Health of Students', Proc. Brit. Stud. Health Assn.

Watts, C. A. H., *et al.* (1964), *Brit. med J.*, 2, 1351.

Weiss, R. J., *et al.* (1965), *Journ. Nerv. and Ment. Dis.*, 141, (2) 240.

WHO (1966), *Technical Report Series*, No. 320.

CHAPTER SIX

Depression and Suicide

DEPRESSION is a killer. As a disorder it destroys incentive, enthusiasm, concentration and interest in life, and as a disease that may be unrelieved it can, by leading to suicide, destroy the life of its sufferer. There is dispute amongst psychiatrists about whether depressive illness can be 'endogenous' (arriving often unheralded by physical disturbance or upset in the social environment) or 'reactive' (when clear reasons can be detected and presumed to be at least to some degree causative). The endogenous type, if the classification is accepted, is the one that more commonly affects the middle-aged and is more severe; the reactive type is, however, more common in the young. It may all in the long-term prove to be a disorder of the body's chemistry anyway, and these behavioural classifications that are now convenient may be outmoded once the biochemistry and physiology of man's most precious asset—the brain—is understood. Notwithstanding any surmise, however, it is certainly true that when the adolescent is depressed there are often many environmental reasons that seem obvious, and if they are not the actual cause, the depression nevertheless can be seen as an understandable reaction to them. Depressive illness also follows—as if it were a state of profound emotional exhaustion—chronic anxiety. Perhaps being in a physical 'alarm' state, sustained without relaxation for too long, produces depression, for certainly when psychotherapeutic interviews are conducted with the depressed adolescent patient there is almost constant evidence of prolonged anxiety, excitement and emotional agitation that preceded the withdrawn, apathetic state of depression. Snyder (Psychiatrist-in-Chief, Massachusetts Institute of Technology, USA) has defined depression as 'a state of psychological helplessness of the ego which can be associated with either overwhelming environmental pressures or overwhelming psychological pressures, or both; a situation in which there is, so to speak, no energy available on demand on the part of the ego'–and for reference to the adolescent the definition can hardly be bettered. Thus the individual student who is a perfectionist in his work to an almost obsessional degree can be constantly making such demands of himself that are so extreme as to be impossible to meet (no student can cope with some reading lists handed out by certain academic departments at the beginning of term), and he is thus constantly smothered with a sense of inadequacy, even though his actual performance may be brilliant according to his tutors. Hence his own self-esteem, which is judged in his terms by these perfectionist demands, is constantly being cut-down and undervalued. An example of dynamic motivation leading to a sense of helplessness and depression. A sense of utter despair can equally be initiated by grief, failure to resolve personal emotional crises over, say, homosexuality, or by the broken engagement where one or other partner blames themselves for imagined inadequacies, physically, psychologically or in an apparent inborn failure to feel sufficiently affectionate. Home-sickness, creating a very real sense of isolation, is commonly experienced by adolescents away from home for the first time. Those who suffer worst are the ones who looked forward to leaving the parental environment, and said so before they left, only to find that little satisfaction and a lot of problems can arise as a result of their new-found freedom and responsibility. Eating 'humble pie' and admitting they were wrong does not come easily in youth. Similarly, even within a country as small as the UK, there are profound regional and cultural differences, and someone from, say, Newcastle, can feel very lonely in Berkshire, whilst a southerner used to warmth and the early

signs of spring in the surrounding countryside can hate the
long-drawn-out winters and dark dirty cities of northern
industrial England. Cultural alienation can be felt even by
indigents of one country. Academic inadequacy is a very real
cause of a depressive illness in the privileged adolescent,
particularly when the individual concerned cannot adjust to
or accept it. Inability to keep up with the class, fear of failure
and disappointing parents, and the lack of any alternative plans
for a career or employment are all frustrations that can drive
the sensitive individual to despair. There are some, of course, who
will in such circumstances welcome with profound relief the
institution's judgement that they are unsuitable – as if they are
submitting themselves to a test for their own satisfaction or in
order to show their parents that their hopes were misplaced –
but others will dread the possibility of being 'weeded out'.
Thus one finds two types of depressed student, the ones who
feel there is something wrong with them, and the ones who feel
there is something wrong with the institution into which they
have been plunged, and in both the stress can produce a
depressive reaction. Some of course will ignore all the pressures
of the academic treadmill on which they find themselves un-
suitably placed and will adjust by developing personal
criteria for success which they strive to achieve by every
means possible. Outlandish social behaviour, sport, drug-
taking, sexual adventures, 'union' activities from politics to
protest can all attract individuals who find satisfaction in these
pursuits having failed to become a leader at study; and it is
too easy to blame the apparently endless list of extra-mural
activities that some patients present with as being the
cause of failure, and not to see them as perhaps the effect.
Then there are the intellectual risk-takers, the undergraduate who neglects, say, the disciplined hard work of the
Anglo-Saxon course for the pleasure and satisfaction of turning
in a top-grade critical essay on poetry, or the post-graduate
who starts on his thesis fired with enthusiasm only to prove, once
the apparatus is set up and the results start being recorded,

that his theory was wrong (and can get no satisfaction from this even though academically it was all a very worth-while piece of work) – these are the ones who frequently react by depression to a backlog of work that they do not like doing, but must complete before finals, or to the realisation that they are not destined to become the Leonardo's or Nobel laureates of their generation.

There is often a paradox, however, in a young person's depression in the academic community – one that is moreover reflected in many ways at all ages – and that is that it is not necessarily the unworthy who consider themselves so. Just as the rich depressive is frightened of poverty, and the successful businessman fears bankruptcy, so the brilliant student will express personal fears of academic inadequacy. To the doctor, teacher or parent, there is a terrible trap in dealing with the depressed, and that lies in taking their word too seriously. The fears can be phobias, the frustration imagined and the reaction grossly exaggerated. The patient who complains he or she cannot cope may have just done a brilliant essay or thesis and yet be personally dissatisfied. Depression may be anguish – a sad, dejected mood that is transient and follows a quite minor (apparently to the observer) frustration or upset in the affairs of the student's life, or it may be a whole syndrome of disturbance character-ised by underactivity and withdrawal, loss of appetite, suicidal ruminations, feelings of hopelessness and early morning insomnia. It may appear to a second person as a mood that is just part of a conscientious and spiritually creative nature; on the other hand it may present as an illness that disables an individual and cuts him off from activity, pleasure and his fellow men, rendering him totally ineffectual in the academic community. We have thus the depressive neurosis, and the psychotic depressive reaction which are both shades of the same disease; both disable to a degree whether socially or academically, and both deserve earnest attention because of their 'snowball' effect on the young academically endowed individual. This effect is where the student worries because he feels depressed and so does no work because of the worry, and then becomes more depressed because he is doing no work. There is a viciousness to the academic destruction that depression can wreak.

The symptomatology is complex, but generally, though not always, obvious. A loss of interest is paramount, whether it is in work, pleasure or the future, and there is often an allied criticism-of-self combined with many vague physical complaints from loss of appetite to constipation, and fleeting pains to dyspepsia, all of which are thrown up to classify the patient as a high 'doctor-usage' candidate, for he or she will be frequently seen in consultation. No satisfying underlying disease process is found for the complaints but this is rarely acceptable to the depressed patient who will return with some other complaint referring to another of the body's systems, once investigation of the former complaint has been completed and found to be negative. The tutor will see a general slowing-up of the intellectual interest and a degree of withdrawal expressed by absence from tutorials or seminars, or flimsy excuses presented for failure to hand in essay work or attend pre-arranged appointments. Sleep gets progressively out of order, with the patient feeling tired all day, falling asleep in the evenings when study should be undertaken, and early morning waking with an inability to return to slumber. This symptom can be seen as part of the withdrawal mechanism and is frequently accompanied by a desire to stay in bed in the mornings 'because I am tired', rather than get up and go to lectures. Apathy is a hall-mark of depression.

Apathy is nevertheless a defence mechanism that protects the patient from being hurt. By living out a role of being deficient, the patient prevents himself from dealing with circumstances that might be painful – intellectually or socially – until forced to. Hostility and anger is directed inwards and expressed in attacks of acute hysteria in the examination room. Screaming, tearful girls who cry out that they cannot write down a single word, or who refuse even to think of something to put down on the answer paper, are fundamentally committing academic suicide. Boys will more often just fail to turn up for the examination on the appointed day. This is not 'examination nerves' but the result of a depressive illness, masked previously in a multitude of ways, or reflected in high consultation rates over the previous years as an undergraduate, and a tutorial recognition of having 'gone off the boil' in the last few terms.

Apathy may also be seen as a positive physical expression, as obesity in the female compulsive over-eater who constantly states she wants to be slim – as personal and deliberate slovenliness and the purposeful buying of second-hand clothes in order to look outrageous despite parental gifts of money to go out and buy a new coat or suit – as sexual experimentation of the most flagrant manner where girls deliberately permit themselves to be used or insist that their casual male partners take no contraceptive precautions and so present pregnant to their medical advisers as if it was an act of 'sexual suicide'. There is a constantly reappearing sign of self-harm in most of their actions from the obvious case where a boy drives his parents' car into a wall or his own car round and round the hockey pitch and provoking disciplinary reaction, to the more obscure but equally deliberate case of the girl who rejects her loved fiancé and becomes promiscuous with boys from the town she met in a coffee-bar.

The same degree of self-harm is seen in suicide, for this is the most flagrant and instantly recognisable symptom of a depression. If an individual is depressed yet still capable enough of reacting, angry enough with himself, or with others, yet reduced to a particular kind of desperate aggression and frustration with everything, and sees no future before him, or only ruination and disgrace, then suicide is the result. It is a cry for help from the 'wounded' and cornered animal. The last desperate throw of the dice.

Adolescent suicides account for about 3 per cent of the

F

total figure for all ages, but it has been estimated that for every teenager who succeeds in taking his own life there are thirty others who make serious suicidal attempts. At the Los Angeles Suicide Prevention Centre two psychologists carried out an investigation into the backgrounds of adolescent girls who made attempts on their own lives, for a period of three years, and many common features emerged. Typically the girls came from emotionally chaotic families, 60 per cent having been brought up in homes broken by divorce or separation. Rightly or wrongly the girls were convinced that their parents—fathers especially—had rejected them because they were social or educational failures. They felt that it was impossible to please their parents, and had come to think that the parents were unconsciously conveying the message 'Everyone would be happier if you were not around'. Thirty per cent of the girls had attempted suicide after rejection by a lover or boy-friend. The mothers of the girls, it was found, had constantly expressed hostile attitudes towards men, warning their daughters that men were insincere, untrustworthy and likely to exploit girls sexually and then abandon them. Some girls saw suicide as the most effective way of punishing their unloving parents, or as a way to compel their parents to accept them and show concern. Others saw it as a form of self-punishment which would expiate their guilt, or else prove their basic goodness. Because many of the girls were suspicious of all adults, then for the therapist there was the constant danger of being viewed as yet another rejecting 'parent'. All these features of adolescent frustration are seen in the academic community and frequently the one major difference that can be added is that girls and boys alike may replace 'parent' by the symbol of the institution. The role they are expected to play by their relatives is replaced by that which they see as expected by their college, university or academic commitment. Thus a number of studies show that the suicide rate of students is (and has remained so for many years) significantly higher than that of the corresponding age group in the general population (see Table I). Whilst women students seem to have suicide death rates typical of the social classes from which they are drawn, there is a preponderance of male suicides in nearly all the studies carried out. Moreover, in the academic community suicide is more likely to occur in term-time (not necessarily in the examination term), and most probably in the first two years at university and not in the final or third year.

There are several social factors that distinguish the privileged adolescent from the general population which are highly relevant to the incidence of suicide. An excess of unmarried individuals, an exaggeration of the effects of depressive neurosis on the life role (i.e. academic work), the conditions of being away from home for long periods (note studies that have revealed higher suicide rates in 'bed-sitter' areas of large towns), in a state of 'role conflict' (i.e. still at school yet an adult, middle-class aspirations yet comparative economic deprivation, a solitary worker in a social milieu and being expected to act as a gregarious student)—all these are loading factors likely to produce an excess of suicides in the student population, by comparison with the world outside the campus. Moreover, living conditions may mitigate against survival from a lonely 'cry for help', for students frequently live alone, in the flat or bed-sitting room, and someone may not be around at the necessary time to turn off the gas or ring the ambulance. The chance of someone intervening is obviously much greater for the young individual who lives at home, or in the hall of residence.

Suicide is also a cultural phenomenon, not just simply in terms of the military person in disgrace or the oriental in defeat, but in terms of being adopted by the privileged adolescent as the most dramatic gesture possible to produce self-harm and hurt to others. Thus suicide is perhaps part of student-life, and whilst the very stresses that produce academic brilliance—the competition that produces the future leaders, administrators and organisers for the community, and the *rites de passage* that every student has to undergo as a self-

TABLE I
SUICIDE RATES IN DIFFERENT CENTRES

Centre	Period	Annual suicide rate per 100,000 of population
England and Wales – ages 15–19	1948–58	1·9
– ages 20–24	1948–58	4·1
Oxford University	1948–58	26·4
Cambridge University	1948–58	21·3
London University	1948–58	16·3
Seven British Universities	1948–58	5·9
State of California, ages 15–41	1952–61	16·01
University of California, Berkeley	1952–61	17·44

TABLE II
SUICIDE RATES FOR
DIFFERENT COUNTRIES IN 1961

Country	Suicide rate per 100,000 population
Hungary	25·4
Austria	21·9
Czechoslovakia	20·6
Finland	20·6
Japan	19·6
England and Wales	11·3
United States	10·5

selected candidate—also produces the casualties, it produces them in a particular manner typical of the group concerned. The sociologist Maxwell Atkinson tested the hypothesis that students see suicide as part of student life by asking fifty of them from one university to write out the kind of story they would expect to find under a given headline in a local paper. The headlines provided were 'Student found dead on campus' and 'Labourer found dead on building site'. Half the sample wrote about one headline and the other twenty-five constructed what they felt would be a typical newspaper paragraph about the other headline. Sixty-four per cent of those writing about the student described or mentioned suicide as the likely cause, only eight per cent considered it as the cause of death for the labourer. This study was little more than an exercise and conclusions too firmly drawn are not necessarily valid, nevertheless it gives some support to the hypothesis that students see suicide as a pattern of behaviour likely to be followed by members of their group. It is going too far to suggest that suicide is a student fashion, but potential suicides are certainly more likely to kill themselves, or try to, if they believe others expect them to do so. Moreover, one might carefully consider what methods and ways there are for the student to 'opt out' of a predicament that personally he or she finds absolutely intolerable. With the responsibility of parental expectation, or cultural demand, the necessary role and obligations required by the institution or academic commitment, the personal crisis of failure to reach the individual's standards, or the self-accusation inherent when any or all of these factors provoke and produce a depressive illness, there really does seem little alternative to self-destruction. The privileged adolescent is after all untrained for any other occupation, and if he cannot adapt to failure in the chosen one, he is perhaps unlikely to be able to seek out another form of employment. In youth there are few 'greys', it is for us all at that time more a matter of 'black' or 'white'.

This is of course conjecture, but then about student suicide there must be much conjecture. It is possible, for example, that selection plays a part; not only the selection methods employed by colleges and universities but also through the operation from early childhood of processes of academic natural selection–the survival to university age of the scholastically fittest. It must also be borne in mind that term-time suicides are associated with the increased seasonal incidence that occurs in many countries during the months of April, May and June– and that, internationally, suicide rates are higher in towns than in rural areas–and the campus is either in, or acts as, a town for the student who originates from a rural district. Difficulties of sexual adjustment are more pronounced in the student population than they are in the general population where marriage, home-making and family rearing are more readily possible as natural outlets. Amongst students anxiety, often unfounded but chronic, about homosexuality seems to be more common than amongst other young people and, for some, despair over this fear has played a crucial part in under-graduate suicide. Finlay has probably performed the most careful analysis of student suicide in his research into twenty years' figures at the University of Leeds, however, and con-jecture is replaced by fact where he revealed a distressing rise in the incidence during the seven years that followed 1960 by comparison with the years before. In this more recent period male and female attempts were found not to be numerically dissimilar (24 men, 28 women), except that there was a ratio of 73 men to 27 women per 100 students, thus giving the female a much greater incidence rate. Nevertheless, men made more successful or serious attempts on their lives more frequently than women, in that death could easily have occurred and did not do so because of some usually chance intervention, whereas in women it was found that the attempt was less serious in general and more 'a cry for love or attention' than an attempt at self-destruction. This pattern detected by Finlay must in-evitably play its part in the international findings of the greater rate of suicide for male than female students. Indigent students rather than those from overseas, who had shown previous instability in health whilst at the university, who in general did not play team games, and tended to belong to the Arts and Sociology faculties (a higher number of women in these faculties) and who gave an unstable family history in the social sense (i.e. lost one or both parents from divorce, separation or death) were found to be the most vulnerable in this survey. Regular church attendance, as a reflection of active religious interest, indicated no difference in risk and neither did a personal history of parent's or sibling's psychiatric breakdown. With regard to precipitating factors, an unhappy love affair ranked equally with academic difficulty or examination stress, and Finlay found that the most common method of suicide chosen was that of self-administered poisoning, with personal violence being relatively uncommon. Any method selected by suicidal individuals, however, is always a reflection of the ease of access, and gassing (the commonest form of room heating at these institutions) is found to be the commonest in the universities of Oxford and Cambridge. There is, nevertheless, a tendency for the schizophrenic student, when he or she attempts suicide, for it to be the most violent and often bizarre method of all. Perhaps when the schizophrenic is hallucinating the natural fear of physical harm is quelled, but certainly self-immolation by setting fire to a petrol-soaked body has become a trend noticeable in recent years amongst those given to excessive religious or political fervour and the suspicion of schizophrenic traits cannot be easily dismissed. There is, however always the point of 'fashion' to be considered and the part that the mass media play in reporting such incidents.

One further point with regard to suicide and method employed needs mention: hanging. Forensically it is well recognised that young and middle-aged males will often seek to obtain a degree of sexual stimulation from experimenting with constrictions round the neck. Loss of consciousness can easily ensue and consequent hanging, and it is by no means rare to find pornographic literature lying round the corpse and for the body to be in a state of undress or clad in female attire. These cases are genuine accidents and not deliberate suicides, although in the reports and coroners' inquests the unsavoury details–out of respect to the family–may be left out.

The academic outcome of the genuinely suicidally-inclined student is poor. A third of the patients studied continued their course, a third achieved a degree ultimately, and the remaining third were either dead or withdrew without a degree.

Given, then, the academically destructive disorder of depression and the possibly lethal consequence of suicide, what can be done to ameliorate the effects and prevent the tragic losses that otherwise occur? The actual number of young men and women who take their lives may be small (between 10 and 20 per 100,000 undergraduate population), although the attempts are more numerous (between 60 and 80 per 100,000 undergraduate population), nevertheless it is an unacceptable price to pay for emancipation, autonomy and academic aspiration. Selective processes have proved unequal to the task of identifying the vulnerable with any degree of accuracy. Student suicide may be preventable by refusing a place to certain applicants with a medical or family history suggestive of risk, or by insisting that their psychiatric supervision is rigorous and thereby one might only displace the figures from 'student' to 'general population' or jeopardise the possible recovery of the individual from the crippling wounds of their childhood. Psychological screening in the UK and America is no longer practised on potential college entrants because it is a very dubious practice with less than minimal value. At best the methods used, such as personality inventory tests and measures of extroversion, introversion, detect only the very overt disorders which need immediate attention, or are already receiving it. Moreover, many of the world's most talented geniuses probably were, and still are, overburdened with neuroses perfectly compatible with pronounced academic brilliance. A medical history, however, obtained from the family

physician of the pre-entrant student can be of invaluable use
where a comprehensive College or University Health Service
exists, as a means not only of identifying the 'risk' cases but also
(when consultation is sought) of 'breaking the ice' in discussing
the patient's previous history. For this to be any value, however
it is necessary for a comprehensive health service to exist for the
students' use, and many writers have suggested that where
these services are found, then consequently there is a lower
suicide rate. This begs the question a little, for a great number
of circumstances may be operating to make one institution's
student different from those of another. The college staircase,
for example–a feature of the architecture at the older
universities of Oxford and Cambridge where rooms are
rather isolated from each other in small blocks–'may
facilitate study but it can lead to loneliness and can encourage
brooding', parental ambition may be greater, the competition
for places may be greater at one institution than another and
fewer of the students may live at home in one than in another
university–many circumstances mitigate for or against
variations in rates between countries and institutions of further
education. It is nevertheless true that the comprehensive
university health services–as distinct from a 'recommended'
college doctor–which provide not only preventive but also
general practitioner medical services for undergraduates, make
it more likely that a student in distress will know of at least
one source of help to which he or she can turn when depression looms or insomnia aggravates.

Similarly, and this is peculiar to the academic environment,
because depression shows in the signs of a work 'fall off', the
tutor can often be the first to suspect a psychological illness in
the student. Indeed the tutorial staff are often the first to
worry about whether the student requires reprimand for
laziness or referral for medical advice, and herein lies the
'umpire' role of the physician involved in the health care of
the privileged adolescent. The decision is not necessarily clear,
but the experienced tutor can recognise apathy, withdrawal and

emotional disturbance as classical signs for concern. The need, therefore, within any academic community is for lines of access and communication to medical advice; counselling can act as a first line of contact, but even the best counsellor cannot cope with a disorder that is characterised by depression and which needs medical treatment.

The medical treatment of emotional disorders in adolescents follows the same modes of treatment as for adults – except perhaps for a justifiable reluctance to use ECT (electroconvulsive therapy) because of the amnesic effects and concentration impairment that follows this form of treatment. For the great majority of adolescents individual or group therapy (and a medical consultation with a physician who has time to listen is), brings them through the critical stage, especially when allied with this 'getting it off the chest' is a prescription for a mild hypnotic or antidepressant preparation – safe in accidental or deliberate overdosage. Many of the modern antidepressants have drowsiness as a side-effect and use can be made of this by prescribing directions that they should be taken at night, thus overcoming the insomnia and alleviating to a degree the depressive reaction. The modern armamentarium of the physician has meant that in general most depressive attacks can be shortened and hospitalisation avoided.

Two features require stressing, however. Firstly that medical treatment is effective – if only because recognition leads to sympathy, someone doing something about the stresses the student is undergoing, and a general concern to alleviate the torture of despair ensuing for the otherwise isolated and withdrawn individual. Secondly, the student is helped to understand and gain 'insight' but must be helped also to appreciate that pills do not solve problems and that adjustment is necessary to avoid future distress or recurrence. It is here that counselling, psychotherapy and group measures are effective. Mental hygiene courses have been tried in the past as protective mental health measures and were widely used twenty years ago in the USA, but their greatest fault was that the lecturer represented a primarily intellectual approach to an apparently isolated occurrence that happened to 'other' people and their value to the sufferer was minimal. In general they have been abandoned, although if this approach is of any use at all, it can be used with effect as instruction for the staff, and not the students – for early recognition of their tutee's symptoms. Group discussions, however, do have their value, particularly when they involve 'social tutorial groups' across the academic years. Examples of effective anticipatory guidance (as used by the preparation courses for the Peace Corps candidates in the USA) are in existence in several medical schools in the UK, where staff members accept a degree of responsibility for entertaining and looking after a student group that has one or more representatives of each academic year. Thus the final student retails the difficulties he is undergoing to the students in the years below, and the staff member also acts as 'moral tutor', to each of his or her brood. Sororiety and fraternity groups in the USA can fulfil similar roles. Contact, in other words, across the anonymity of the undergraduate years and between staff and student, goes far to mitigate the effects of isolation and provides a ready samaritan service to the student in difficulty.

Finally, active therapeutic intervention, readily available on the campus by those experienced in dealing with adolescents or familiar with the peculiar stresses of their academic environment, is the only hope for the amelioration of depression or the reduction in the incidence of self-harm in the academic community. The Dean of Freshmen students at Harvard has made a particularly cogent comment on the problem regarding the ever-present need for skilled medical and psychiatric help to college students with the statement: 'With so many wonderful kids on the beach it pays us to have capable life-guards at hand.' An adolescent has to learn to swim in the sea of experience, but that he should drown while trying to is an avoidable tragedy.

Bibliography and Further Reading

Braceland, F. J., and Farnsworth, D. L. (1969), *Maryland. Med. Journ.*, 18, (4), 67.

Davy, B. (1964), *J. Med. Women's Fed.*, 46, (3), 166.

Douglas, J. D. (1967), *The Social Meaning of Suicide*, Princeton Univ. Press, New Jersey.

Finlay, S. E. (1968), Proc. Brit. Stud. Health Assn.

Gundle, S. (1968), 'Protection of Mental Health in Univ. of the USA', *Stud. Health News*, 5.

Kobler, A. L., and Stotland, E. (1964), *The End of Hope*, Free Press, New York.

Kolb, L. C. (1965), *Aspects of Depressive Illness*, Livingstone, London.

Maxwell Atkinson, J. (1968), *Social Rev.*, 16, 83.

—— (1969), *Univ. Quart.*, Spring, 213.

Munton, A. (1968), *Student*, 3, 13.

Odlum, D. (1963), *Journey through Adolescence*, Penguin, London.

Porter, A. M. W. (1970), *Brit. med. J.*, 1, 773.

Rook, A. F. (1954), *Brit. med. J.*, 1, 773.

Roth, M. (1968), Proc. Brit. Stud. Health Assn.

Seiden, R. H. (1966), *Journ. Ab. and Soc. Psychol.*, 71, 389.

Slater, E., and Sheilds, J. (1967), Paper given at Symposium on Anxiety, Documenta Geigy, London.

Snyder, B. R. (1968), Proc. Brit. Stud. Health Assn.

Stengel, E. (1964), *Suicide and Attempted Suicide*, Penguin, London.

Toolan, S. M. (1962), *Amer. J. Psychiat.*, 118, 719.

Usdin, G. L. (1967), *Adolescent Care and Counselling*, Lippincott, Philadelphia and Toronto.

CHAPTER SEVEN

The Special Problems of the Foreign Student

THE DEVELOPED nations might be seen to have a debt to those other nations, which were often former colonies and which are now struggling to emerge into the sophisticated technological age of the twentieth century and a debt that can be repaid in educational terms. Lacking adequate primary and secondary educational processes, these countries' problems are even greater when it comes to adult, further or tertiary education. Universities and colleges in the underdeveloped countries are largely staffed by expatriates, their students are a specific élite privileged often only by their family's economic background and they probably reflect today, through no fault of their own, the situation that existed in European society some fifty years ago. A country with a poor and underdeveloped economy cannot afford free-for-all education, and yet ironically it is probably only through this that the economy and administration of the country can be lifted up to its rightful position. There are financial problems and selection difficulties because the student from the underdeveloped country must be able to compete equally with his European or American colleague, nevertheless, by comparison with other countries, the UK does not seem to be offering an equal share of its places in tertiary education (see Chapter One). This is unfortunate, because it can be readily appreciated that to train doctors,

93

lawyers, engineers, architects and administrators for a country, and send them back to pioneer and lead their own countrymen, is a better form of 'aid' than money, which can be more easily abused by an inadequate administration.

Nevertheless, the 'foreign' students seen in most universities are invariably a mixture of Europeans, Americans, Africans, students from the near and Far East with a few – often post-graduate – from Canada, Australia, New Zealand and other Commonwealth countries. (See Tables I, II and III.) The psychological problems of all students of course include prolonged dependence on parents, their temporary status and insecurity at an age when other social groups already enjoy clearly defined social and professional status, identity crises

TABLE I

OVERSEAS STUDENTS IN UK

	University	All others (approx.)	Total (approx.)	Total number all students at University overseas and UK
1950–51	8,242	4,258	12,500	80,602
1954–55	9,050	15,950	25,000	—
1958–59	10,672	31,428	42,100	104,009

TABLE II

OVERSEAS STUDENTS DISPERSAL IN UK

	University	Technical Colls.	Nursing Students	All others* (approx.)	Total (approx.)
1959–60	11,001	11,944	5,850	18,725	47,520
1964–65	14,981	16,724	14,526	22,243	68,474
1968–69	15,975	13,798	16,356	23,690	69,819

* Inns of Court, Colleges of Ed., Practical Training, and other institutions, including private colleges.

TABLE III
COUNTRIES SENDING LARGEST NUMBERS OF STUDENTS,
1967–8; TO THE UK

USA	2,078	2,018
India	1,568	1,429
Pakistan	981	899
Canada	818	784
Norway	692	678
Nigeria	789	641
Malaysia	657	597
Australia	499	480
Iraq	464	423
Kenya	463	386

and adaptation to new learning methods–but for the foreign student every one of these problems is accentuated and inevitably of greater emphasis. They are away from their homes and their loved ones in a foreign society with different cultural patterns of behaviour and they labour under the burden of responsibility for success in order to live up to the prestige and expectations of those at home. People spending a certain time abroad and supposed to return later–garlanded with academic honours–often arrive in their host country with exaggerated expectations. On encountering difficulties their morale and self-confidence diminish rapidly, leading to disillusion and exceptional home-sickness. Their mental equilibrium improves however, in parallel with the extent to which they can adapt–and it may be that they are helped considerably by coming from an English-type society to an English-speaking society, for certainly the more 'native their background the greater the difficulties they experience,' not least with adapting to the landlady's fish and chips instead of their customary curry. The postgraduate trainees face added problems, for they are probably already married with young families just starting, and they have to leave them and take up the life of the lonely bachelor in a foreign country. If they are wealthy, then by bringing the family they avoid many of the personal health problems they would otherwise suffer – but at considerable expense, and they often then face housing difficulties.

Another aspect of the overseas students' problems concerns the preconceived ideas in the host country about aliens. Racial and cultural prejudice exists in every country throughout the world, and the dislike of black for the apparently parasitic white ruling class in one country is matched by the prejudice of indigent white for coloured foreigners in another. These not only affect student milieux and teaching personnel, but also landladies, sexual partners and members of the public met in ordinary life outside the academic institution. A large number of damaging reactions may result. Xenophobia is never pleasant. Where hostel accommodation is not available, the foreign student may be exposed to genuine tyranny on the part of landladies (in Austria this is reported by Strotzka (1965) as being one of the main causes of psychological problems in foreign students), or else forced to put up with substandard accommodation in the 'twilight' areas of the large industrial towns, living in circumstances of the widest disparity to those he or she would be used to 'at home'. They may be victims of financial exploitation and suffer inadequate lighting, heating and space or facilities for study, and in the area in which they live meet only the uneducated lower socio-economic classes of their host country. In term-time the routine of the academic institution takes them out of this, and often they will return to their lodgings only to sleep, having, by day, studied in the College Library and eaten in the Students' Union – but in the vacation they are left to their own devices (except for the auspices of some excellent voluntary organisations and in the UK the British Council) and may become exceptionally lonely, when all their friends have 'gone down'. Among one of the more dangerous consequences of this situation is that of meeting with sexual partners of inadequate social standard. The 'town girl' may be their only sexual contact and as such perhaps offer them a distorted view for life of the culture in which they find themselves 'guests'. The incidence of gonorrhoea and other veneral infection is high in the UK amongst the immigrant males who have not got their families with them, and this is not necessarily a criticism of them, only a mark of their social isolation and a criticism of the poverty of the social contact available.

Frequently foreign students arrive without sufficient knowledge of the host-country language. The result may sometimes be a neurotic reaction of discouragement. Many students think they can learn the language on the spot but never succeed, or they become academically so behind, because they cannot understand the lecturer's accent, that they suffer in their undergraduate career a permanent disability. Language problems in a more subtle way complicate counselling, medical advice and psychotherapy. Even if the foreign student understands the teaching language well enough to study, it may still be very difficult to make him understand, for instance, that there may be a relation between his hypochondriacal symptoms and his psychological problems. The same, too, applies in the diagnosis and treatment of somatic diseases. There is often a vast cultural gulf to bridge; for example, many overseas students will regard any oral therapy say with antibiotics, as inadequate, because they have always been treated at home by injection—they paid more for an injection course than tablets, and therefore it was 'better medicine'. Similarly, herbal remedies purchased over the chemist's counter may be seen as more 'powerful' than the physician's prescription which is left uncollected in the drawer. Experience at the Lumumba University in Moscow has shown that a special staff acquainted with the students' respective language, background and culture is necessary to overcome these problems that occur when there are large numbers of overseas students to care for.

The impossibility of obtaining his habitual food may not only cause the student real somatic problems—and every physician is familiar with the newly arrived's dyspepsia—but

G

contribute considerably to homesickness. Differences of climate may not only affect the student physically and mentally—although there is often joy at the first sight of snow to match the depression of the temperate climate's continual drizzle and fog—but also call for an expensive outlay on clothing. It is the African student whose chest the physician wants to examine, who takes the longest to undress as layer after layer of sweaters (sometimes worn below the shirt) have to be peeled. Religious difficulties arise, and a period spent as a student in a foreign land may produce the first separation of the individual from his beliefs, with a consequent aggravation of any insecurity. Foreign students may be either poor, or the victims of excessive generosity, financially, from their families or governments. In either case at each extreme their difficulties in integration with the local student milieu will be accentuated. Neither the tinted-windowed Mercedes parked next to the students' scooters, nor the financial inability to visit and explore the countryside or national parks are likely to lead to ready acceptance by other students. They may also face a change in learning techniques from what they are used to. In many countries during the high-school or secondary education period it is considered and taught to be more important to learn by heart than really to understand everything, while at the university of the country of reception the accent may be on comprehension rather than memorisation. Many foreign students are not informed early enough that this is so, but then they may also originate from an educational system that is inadequately staffed and not geared to different forms of imparting knowledge.

Such social difficulties may aggravate and distort an initial phase of discouragement on arrival in the host country, and the student needs to compensate in one way or another. Exaggerated attention to language and housing difficulties—even though they are real—delays the attention to studies. There may be a mental crisis owing to their sense of duty to their home country, or an overwhelming sense of inferiority.

The opposite may be seen with megalomanic concepts of their own person or country of origin and acute distress blamed as being due to a whole host of (psychosomatic) symptoms. Subsequently, as with all frustration, there may be aggression – in attitudes to their hosts, or their country of origin, blaming those at home for depriving them of the ability to compete. This is turn may make them interrupt all links with their home country and try to establish roots in the host country. At best they may be successful and overcome the problems of prejudice, mixed marriage and frustration in employment; at worst they may be forced home, embittered and bearing a permanent grudge against the society and country that, they feel, rejected them.

From their vulnerability to social hazard perhaps stems their increased morbidity to physical disease, or at least a higher consultation rate. Principally digestive troubles, with a degree of heightened proneness to infection with upper respiratory viruses, the morbidity pattern almost invariably reflects their difficulties with self-medication and self-nursing. Tropical disease may be present (from malaria to intestinal infestation) or diseases such as tuberculosis, which are rare in the host environment but more common in their home. Those who originate from humid climates often suffer a pruritis of the skin, which may show an icthyotic or scaling pattern, and it can be intensely irritable. It is probably due to lack of sweat and skin-oil stimulus, plus a heightened degree of skin-moisture removal by the dry cold winds. It soon settles after acclimatisation, with the addition of topical therapy – but it may be seen, interestingly enough, as the reverse condition of 'prickly heat'.

Most who are experienced in their care agree that there is an elevated incidence in the psychopathological symptoms observed in foreign students (18 per cent of all such students, in France for example, consult the Mental Health services during their stay) and that the nature of their symptoms differs widely from that seen in the local population. There is no doubt that the cultural background of the patient contributes to this difference. There is a preponderance of psychosomatic, hypochondriac and hysterical symptoms, particularly in those who originate from the underdeveloped countries. Disturbed sexuality–especially impotence–and paranoia feature prominently. Local students in contrast to them, and in common with European and American students, usually seem to suffer more typical psychoneurotic disorders of disturbed concentration, anxiety neuroses and obsessional or phobic symptoms. Moreover many African and Asian students find a psychological (instead of a physical) explanation of their symptoms completely incomprehensible, and they will insist on somatic treatment in spite of their being proven by laboratory test to be in all respects physically healthy.

One of the many reasons for these minor disorders (which may be acutely important from the work-disturbance point of view) is their relations with sexual partners. They may as students, be older than their local colleagues but undergo the same drives, desires and appetites as the more youthful since perhaps–and it is a common experience to all races–sexuality is heightened by being a long way from home. They may, as a consequence, find themselves in serious conflict with the moral laws of their home country, changing from a very strict milieu based on caste or status, into an apparently liberal one, in which, however, it generally turns out that it is only the ways in which the taboos are observed that are different. This leads to guilt and disturbance, psychologically. Moreover, the foreign student is not always able to estimate the real social and personal qualities of the partner chosen, which may lead to a degree of social isolation from their colleagues and subsequently failure or wastage, if not a life-long contempt for the females of the host country.

Students from overseas are more prone than local ones to react with psychogenic symptoms to stress situations that occur in the initial 'settling in' period and later during examinations– as if, once enabled to adapt, they manage well after integration until the time of competitive 'weighing' in the academic balance approaches. Those who are unable to adapt, fail, or undergo secondary more serious changes (e.g. alcoholism in the South Americans in Spain, drug addiction in Switzerland), with so-called psychotic disease intervening. It is particularly difficult at times, for example, for a psychiatrist to differentiate psychogenic 'emotional crises' in a person from a totally foreign culture from apparent schizophrenia, and when true mental disability occurs it is particularly unfortunate. In these somewhat rare cases repatriation offers the best hope of recovery. Where breakdown is total, however, there is a double tragedy, a combination of failure in selection with failure in support— and for the individual concerned their return home is again an acknowledgement of their mission's failure in the eyes of the society that sent them. Unhappiness during their stay is obviously not so bad, if, like victorious gladiators, they return with the academic spoils of success—but nevertheless, as hosts, every country often fails the foreign student in some way. If the enterprise of redeeming our debt and truly helping them is to be undertaken, then there is an undoubted need, too often unfulfilled, for the country that invites them as a guest to see they receive the continued hospitality and care they rightly deserve.

Bibliography and Further Reading

Berger, W. (1966), *Ostrr. Hochschulzeitung*, **18**, 8.

Berner, P. (1967), 'Student Health Services', Report on Symposium at Cracow. WHO, Copenhagen.

Commonwealth Univ. Year Book (1969), UGC, London.

Donon Boileau, H., *et al.* (1965), *Rev. Hyg. Med. Soc.*, 13, (2), 177.

Gifford, P. W. W. (1961), Proc. Brit. Stud. Health Assn.

Read, J. C. (1959), *Med. World*, 90, 18.

Royal Coll. of Physicians (1966), Report of Social and Preventive Medicine Committee, London.

Strotzka, H. (1965), *Münsch. med. Wschr.*, 107, (34), 1598.

WHO (1966), *Technical Report Series*, No. 320.

CHAPTER EIGHT

The Revolt of the Privileged

'In short we are impatient and suffer from an excess of idealism.' Letter in *The Times*, London, January 30, 1969.

STUDENT PROTEST is a new phenomenon. Riotous behaviour is not, for there have always been the carnivals, rags, boat-race suppers and orgies of temporary anti-social but comparatively harmless, 'horse-play' that have been known popularly since Chaucer's day as 'high-spirits'. It is only in recent years, however, that student riots have become student revolt. Viewed analytically, or epidemiologically, the outbreaks that have become common news in the last three or four years seem to share certain features:

(1) They arise in privileged, not underprivileged groups, in that the prestige universities would seem quite possibly to be affected most (e.g. Berkeley, Harvard, Prague, Mexico, LSE and Essex, Oxford, Paris, Tokio).

(2) They associate strongly with the grievances of the underprivileged (ghettos, housing, Vietnam-fighters, underpaid-workers, etc.) as if those who are involved bear a 'burden of guilt' for their privilege.

(3) They are fundamentally anti-authority whether against political, academic, legal, parental, papal or governmental power structures.

(4) The ardour of their protest seems to be both out of proportion to the complaint, and unpredictably violent,

as if repression only creates a greater energy of protest. Student revolt is not lightly dismissed.

Thus in France and Indonesia they virtually brought about the fall of governments, in California they have almost totally disrupted the academic institutions for a year, and in Japan dramatically affected the foreign policy of the country's government. Ringleaders may be labelled as 'thugs of the academic world', and with regard to public feeling student protest tends to achieve a feeling of alienation, righteous indignation and a disproportionate desire for cutting down on educational expenditure. The UK spends more than £260 million a year on university education but the attitudes of the recipients may be reflected by the comment from the letter to *The Times* quoted above: 'Finally the taxpayer should realise that in financing our studies he is not buying our souls.' There is no sense of obligation or servile gratitude for privileges by the adolescent of today.

Why should this new phenomenon have arisen? Is it because we cannot expect to teach the young the mistakes of the older generations and hope they will not want to change the *status quo*? Is it because society is unable to cater for the creativity and enthusiasms of youth–that has perhaps in the past been masked by war, unemployment, physical deprivation or economic depression? Does well-fed, healthy youth in a socialised environment experience emptiness and desolation at the thought of the roles it must fulfil in the adult society of today? There are more questions than answers in the consideration of student protest, and this in itself is perhaps significant.

Perhaps the cause of social malaise starts earlier in childhood and education than is often appreciated. Child-rearing practices have increasingly become child-centred, particularly among the middle classes. 'Feeding on demand' is perhaps followed by family practices which are geared to the children's satisfactions until formal education takes over. Nowadays the stimulus of creativity is all-important in primary education, but secondary education becomes obsessed with academic competitiveness; here there is an inhibition of the imaginative processes and a replacement by the need to learn and perform well in what are too often memorising capacity tests. Subject specialisation is assumed early, in order to produce better results, and there is a demand for conformity just at the age when there is the greatest disparity in physical and intellectual development. The conformist reproduction of knowledge in examination systems tends to repress the creative and the imaginative, but they are nevertheless aware of the need to succeed and driven on in the hope that the next stage of their education may be more satisfying. There then develops a combination of exaggerated expectations, along with a feeling of anger and rebellion against 'the system' when it is found to be little different from what they experienced at school.

There is another feature, perhaps too little commented upon, and this is that many adolescents—indeed the great majority—seem to pass the standard hurdles of the educational system with personal satisfaction and enjoy their self-chosen vocational training. Those taking up medicine, science, engineering, mathematics and the technologies know that they can expect consistency from the world and they are certain of their career and role in adult society. They may have grumbles about the 'system', but each stage is visualised as a 'rung on the ladder' leading to where they want to be, so the faults of the system may be accepted in the spirit of sacrifice as a price to pay for what they know will be their future reward. This degree of 'role satisfaction' is also reflected in the lower incidence of unwanted pregnancy, 'drop-out', and neurosis—all of these are higher in those studying the non-vocational subjects than they are amongst those enrolled for subjects which led to a specific career in adult society.

Often non-conformist late adolescents are found among those individuals who are unsure of their ultimate role in society. They are under greater social stress than those who know what their place is to be, however consistent their pattern of education may have been. They may, as late developers, have had less time to adjust to the onset of adulthood and may intellectually or imaginatively prefer to undertake the study of subjects such as sociology or psychology because they hope that this will answer their own curiosity about themselves – and then find that these subjects, like any other scientific practice, demand such disciplines as mathematical skill, statistics and ordered thought. The university may then be seen as a hostile authority structure. Staff, separated by the anonymity of large classes, may seem arrogant and disinterested to the puzzled, dissatisfied, unhappy and frustrated individual. Alienated individuals are particularly likely to attack authority figures as symbols of the institutionalisation they resent, and many a college principal, dean, professor or warden has been taken aghast at the enmity they find they can personally inspire.

There are many social forces at work too, for the much quoted 'generation gap' inspires its degree of anger on both sides. The young are treated to inconsistency by the old. Having given their children opportunities they never had themselves, parents may then envy the freedom they see their young enjoying: having taught them to think for themselves they are then anxious about their willingness to conform. Experiencing doubt about their abilities as parents, they are baffled by the reluctance of their adolescents to take notice of them. When small groups of students protest – about anything from factory-farming to racial prejudice – all the adult anxieties of society are focused up them. The media of press, TV and radio distort the true significance and extent of the protest until its proportions snowball. Students and others attend a meeting to see what will happen and the spectator becomes protestor in the eyes of the outsider. Moreover, there is a healthy adventurous desire for horse-play which soon becomes hooliganism and thence direct anti-social violence. Instead of collecting policeman's helmets or beer-mats, they will pull a horse-rider out of the saddle and smash the windows of the pub. Frustration bursts out of all groups into aggression and repressions of even the crowd-controlling police are not necessarily all that easy to inhibit. The incidents in Chigago and Grosvenor Square, London, reflect this problem. A riot is the outcome of emotional force and is therefore a highly-charged, irrational and unpredictable incident. There is also a crowd contagion at work with sinister undercurrents that lead to destruction, injury to people and property, and damage which no one single individual participant would ever normally envisage themselves producing alone, if unaffected by crowd hysteria.

It is this infectious hysteria which permits any hard core of activists, nihilists or shiftless drop-outs to extend their emotional outbursts to involve the otherwise rational. Having been degraded by 'the system' and perhaps having lost their élite status they won merely by gaining a university place, their insecurities can be replaced by a 'gang-leadership' role. All students are reared in a system which rewards merit by restricting continued membership of the system to those who achieve success, in terms of the traditional values of learning. This system processes, packages and labels them, apparently for life, as human resources for the world of industry and commerce, marking them 'pass' or 'failure'. Those marked 'failure' have an inevitable bitterness, because they have lent themselves to this fraud, and been rejected. In the absence of any coherent system for rehabilitation then, they are reduced to incoherent militancy and the rejection of all other systems of order or conformity. As was written on the walls of one university: 'If the system stinks–disrupt it'.

The student demonstration may often start as a justifiable protest at the apparent arbitrariness of the university system–with dissatisfaction with the curriculum as well as with disciplinary rules–and a long overdue reaction against misplaced paternalism. This attitude of authority in the academic campus is traditional and exercised through a body of rules and powers designed fundamentally to protect the student. The college feels in *loco parentis*, and therefore in attempting to fulfil that role attracts the same enmity and rejection as do the *parentes naturales*. It is anachronistic anyway – not only because the adolescent of today has developed physically and physiologically earlier than previous generations but also because their own families have, by the time their young reach the age of 18 or 19, ceased to attempt to 'rule' them. If barriers on the campus have to fall, the first ones are those that restrict, unnecessarily, personal freedom. Most are probably indefensible when they are subjected to careful analysis in any case – rules about guests in bedrooms should perhaps be better based on what the safety and comfort of the community dictates, and not what the warden wants, attendance at lectures should perhaps depend on the 'customers' choice, not the desires of the academic staff, and laboratories could be open for 'convenient' use, not wastefully closed from 5 p.m. onwards. Time-tables might offer choice, not regimentation, and 'consultation' is of the utmost importance. As the Secretary of State for Education and Science has said in Parliament: 'There is a unique change today, however, and this is in the attitude (of the student) towards authority. Young people today will no longer accept old authoritarian concepts of authority when it is imposed by one person on another – whether it is in school, at home, in college or anywhere else. They will only accept authority if they are involved in it, and rightly so.' They belong to a generation which is inclined to question most statements, most rules and most beliefs, no matter how hallowed by time. Many teachers, of course, are delighted to meet this critical attitude – others are not.

There is an important lesson for authority in appreciating the causes embraced by the protesting young, for with critical analysis comes the ability not only to handle the outbursts but also to prevent their occurrence sensibly. Shortly after the London School of Economics affair, Dr. William Boyd, Vice Chancellor of Student Affairs at California University, drew a moral from his experiences at Berkeley for university administrators in Britain. 'Listen to students,' he urged. 'I mean really listen. If we do not listen they are going to find some other way to attract our attention. There are very legitimate needs in the new student population, and if legitimate means are not found for meeting these legitimate ends, then illegitimate means will be resorted to.' Unless moderate student leaders are supported, therefore, they will almost certainly be replaced by a more militant group of leaders whose means of provoking authority to do something will be different. One of the more articulate militants in the UK has stated in public, for example, that inspiration is derived from Cuba, China and the American 'new left', and that as far as his group is concerned, 'Student power means absolute student control–and that means teachers as well– over everything. Our central objective is the democratisation of institutions, such as factories, so that they are controlled by their members. Student representation on governing bodies is only the beginning and representation can be good or bad– it can give a false sense of unity. The next thing is for students to begin to run their own courses, initially through their own societies–and then to demand that they should run a particu- lar part of a course: its content, and how it is taught and who teaches it. I accept the word militancy, but it means for me that one is prepared to consider any action that will achieve one's end, which is in accordance with one's ends. One does not rule out any mode of action because it has not been accepted in the past.' This is not necessarily an 'either-or' situation, because this kind of opinion reflects more the attitude of those who are totally frustrated in their attempts to obtain proper and effective consultation, rather than the view of the majority of students.

Curiously enough it is not just the student population of the university that is unique in feeling a frustration with current academic *modus vivendi*, but also to some extent the staff. They probably stem from a highly educated middle-class background themselves, having been the former élite whose parents could

afford to send them to college, or else were the privileged of
the early post-war years, completing their education with the
maturity of wartime or Services' experience, and nowadays
they too are under direct pressure to conform to the exigencies
of a bureaucratised industry. Large classes, ever accelerating and
agrandising teaching schedules, and involvement in the computer
revolution, the new technologies and the apparatus of social
economic and academic planning – these are challenges that
are new and to a considerable degree upsetting to the
accustomed routines of academic staff. There is a crisis about the
assumption by many students and staff that the universities
have a political and moral role in society and its lack of
definition. A 'degree factory' or an 'ivory tower' is an
unresolved dilemma. There is dissatisfaction with student
motivation, academic standards, work loads, salaries, and the
political in-fighting that goes on continually between departments. The formal and informal processes of communication, as any institution stretches, suffer, and there is a very
evident need for the analysis of not only the attitudes and
aspirations of students themselves, but also the exploration of
the institutional and organisational structure of universities
and colleges and an assessment of their effectiveness and
efficiency. This should be combined with a definition of the
principles of participation and the role of university people,
staff and students alike, in the structure of contemporary
society. Industry complains about the lack of suitable graduates
to employ, and about the inadequacies of their training when
it gets them; teaching is perhaps too often taken up as an option
by the poorer (academically) student who has failed to secure
what he or she wanted in commerce, and the communi-
cations between the academic society and the community are
poor. There is, with the rapidly growing numbers, a greater
need than ever before, for properly equipped and staffed
Appointments Bureaux, to act as the 'eyes and ears' of the
academic institution. Too often have postgraduates returned from
other employment to the haven of the university because they

found that industrial or commercial expectations (or exploitation) of them was greater than they could meet; and the
dissatisfaction was mutual. If we look upon our tertiary
educational facilities in the modern society as anything other
than 'intellectual greenhouses', then we must define the work
of an organisation that is set up to 'process people'. We must examine the role of the student as a client of the professional body
of academic teachers, determine their responsibilities as the group
for whom the university exists (and therefore its most powerful
section) and equate them perhaps as the 'workers' in an
institution more and more closely modelled on the world of
industry for which they are being prepared, and in which the
university staff are seen as the management and the institution
as the employers. University members are the refugees from
parental pressure and the exigencies of the occupational world,
a privileged élite, and the alienated victims of a society in which
the educational system has become the inevitable servant of
industrialism, bureaucracy and technological progress. In
countries like the UK there are more than a million people
involved – staff, students and administrators – and we are used to
unrest in large industries. It should therefore be no surprise to
find it in the academic community.

> 'The universal and chief cause of . . . revolutionary feeling . . .
> is the desire of equality, when men think that they are equal
> to others who have more than themselves; or again the desire
> of inequality and superiority, when conceiving themselves to
> be superior they think that they have not more but the same
> or less than their inferiors.'
>
> Aristotle, *Politics*

Perhaps protest is not such a new phenomenon after all.
Nevertheless it is a new 'fashion' in the university and college
community. The concentration of the media of communication no doubt aggravate its occurrence by the distortions
of publicity – few 'sit-ins' fail to receive press attention and
others soon copy what they have read about as happening

elsewhere–even so the ferocity and damage seen internationally in the larger protests are serious grounds not only for alarm but also for the authorities to totally rethink their methods of dealing with them. Escalation is not confined to Vietnam, and a protest of students that is totally out of hand is a very different matter from crowd control. A student is intelligent, cunning and dangerous in anger because he or she may react like an overgrown child in a tantrum. Petrol bombs and flame-throwers are not the tools of the rationally protesting, and society has need of protection from the damage to person and property that ensues when a student riot 'boils over.' Victimisation and revenge with harsh punishments are ineffective deterrents and only inspire a more vicious reaction. If the police use batons, then the students throw bricks and bottles, tear-gas is answered with fire bombs and so the escalation proceeds. The only answer is prevention. Listening to the requests, consultation across the table, representation and movement towards responsibility are the only acceptable ways of preventing disturbance–patience is the virtue which overcomes protest. In paediatric terms every child learns 'how far to go' by the reaction of the adult–growing up is the acceptance of responsibility. It is as hard for the student to understand the frustrations of the adult world as it is for the adult to appreciate the frustrations of adolescence–but both must, or simple conflict soon becomes serious conflagration.

Bibliography and Further Reading

Adelstein, D. (1969), reported in *The Times*, March 18, London.
Berryman, J. (1969), Letter to *The Times*, Jan. 30, London.
Burns, T. (1968), *Soc. Science Res. Council Newsletter*, 4, Nov.
Editorial (1968), 'Student Unrest', 2, 170.
Etzioni, A. (1965), 'Social Analysis as a Sociological Viewpoint', *AJS*, March 24.
Gibbens, T. C. N. (1966), *Brit. med. J.*, 2, 695.

Parliamentary Reports, *Hansard* (1969), Jan. 30.
Report of the Roy. Comm. on Medical Education (1968), HMSO, London.
Ryle, A. (1968), *Trans. Soc. Occup. Med.*, 18, 28.
Stewart, G. T. (1969), *Lancet*, 1, 617.
Walker Commission Report (1968), 'Rights in Conflict', Nat. Comm. on Causes and Prevention of Violence, Washington, DC.

CHAPTER NINE

The 'Drug Scene'

THE ATTITUDE of the adult community to drugs is like the Victorian attitude to sex, one of covering up, distrust, ignorance, inhibition and fear. It is a paradox in a divorce-prone, tobacco-smoking, alcohol-drinking and sleeping-pill taking society that the adolescent's exploration of sensation—whether the body's senses as with sex, or the psychological perceptions as with various pharmacological substances—should receive such ferocious condemnation. That the developing youth should feel a need for 'escape' from the society he sees himself being plunged into is perhaps more a condemnation of the society than of the youth. But then the older generation has ever been prone to a judgement of its young—which is tainted by the guilt of its own experience.

The misuse of drug substances by adolescents is international. In London coffee bars it may be amphetamine-type stimulants, in Scandinavia strong alcohol, in other European towns glue-sniffing or inhaling paint-thinners are serious problems, whilst in California marihuana and LSD feature prominently in the 'hippie' cultures. The greater ease of travel to the Near East and North Africa has meant that marihuana is also a common European feature of adolescent life, whilst in the UK particularly the misuse of 'pep' pills by adolescents seems to have followed historically and directly the widespread prescription of them by the medical profession for their obese, depressed and unhappy parents. (In 1960 it was estimated that at least two people in every thousand in one

large northern England town were depending on amphetamine preparations. These were mainly married women in
the age group 36–45. Five years later (1965) over 100 million
amphetamine tablets were still being prescribed annually in
Britain. The evidence of their misuse has, however, led to a
gross curtailment of the present-day prescriptions.)

The adolescent is exceptionally vulnerable to the misuse
of any drug, and to dependence upon its effect for solace,
comfort, confidence or escape. There is a liability to total
involvement with the experience and with the group or
the community who use drugs for whatever purpose. There is
a relief to be gained perhaps from the stress of adolescence – or a
sensual pleasure which gives them a feeling of daring, or of
being unique and rejecting adult standards. They will conform in
being society's non-conformists. There is a danger, however,
that those who are least sure of their capacity to be independent
are the ones who are also most likely to take drugs for
relief from their stress–and so therefore the most likely to
become dependent on them. Drugs may be taken in defiance
of the adult community or in imitation of them. The cigarette
may be a symbol of adulthood but the 'reefer' is a group
experience which they alone share. 'The standard thing is to
feel in the gut that middle-class values are all wrong, like the
way America recognises that Communism is all wrong'.
Hallucinogenic substances offer the knives that cut the knots of
an adolescent's feeling 'up-tight' about sex, college, thermo-
nuclear war, Vietnam, parents and the so-called 'standards' of
the adult world–just as alcohol eases the social tension of the
grown-ups' situations and the cigarette is lit by the chronic
bronchitic who is permanently worried about his respiratory
invalidism, but cannot break the habit.

It is dependence or habituation which is the danger with any
experience, from drugs to being superstitious, and this is *par
excellence* the crux of any drug problem in adolescence. Where
a personality is immature there is the greatest of risks of warping
its developments–and even the most enthusiastic protagonists

of 'legalising' marihuana would hesitate to suggest that small children should be enabled to smoke it. Thus the adolescent must be seen as being in need of some protection from the pharmacological hazards of the world at large for three reasons. Firstly, their development, emotionally and psychologically, is incomplete; secondly, all persistent drug misuse carries with it inevitably crippling personality deterioration; and thirdly, the already unstable personality may be precipitated into permanent mental ill-health.

In the university or college community serious drug abuse is not the problem that it is for the community outside the campus—for one relatively simple reason. That is that drug dependence is virtually incompatible with an academic career. Experience with marihuana is no doubt much greater than is generally appreciated—surveys amongst students have shown that up to 40 per cent of UK undergraduates have at some time smoked it, or been offered it, but even this, in the author's opinion, is an underestimate. In the USA the incidence is reportedly much higher, but nevertheless marihuana is a hallucinogenic that does not have true dependence-provoking characteristics. The use of amphetamine-like preparations is not common amongst the privileged adolescents of the UK but, surprisingly perhaps, where it is, it tends to be a lower socio-economic class characteristic and to have started before entry to university or college—a finding which supports the view that more attention needs to be paid to this problem in schools. The stimulants' use confers no advantage to the student academically, and is more liable in fact to result in a deterioration of fine degrees of perceptivity, thus the habituated user tends eventually to disappear from the academic community as a failure, or else to give up their use. The addiction to opiates in the student community is exceptionally rare and about as frequent as true psychosis (less than one in a thousand) which may well be a statistic not without relevance and comparative significance. In view of the personality deterioration inevitably seen with opiate addiction, it is not surprising to find so few in the academic community. The possibility of maintaining a place in an intellectually competitive society whilst being dependent on a regular 'fix' is essentially remote. LSD and other profound hallucinogenics are probably less rare in their use in the UK and European student communities, but there is a degree of exaggeration, nevertheless, about the incidence of all drug-taking and LSD in particular. Non-drug-taking adolescents will have friends who are taking drugs (albeit one 'reefer' in a party shared with twelve others) and because they perhaps enjoy the excitement of this at secondhand they may well exaggerate the number of people involved. The claim to have been 'on a trip' may be presented to the medical adviser as a deliberate attempt to provoke a reaction, or be offered by a latent schizophrenic as an imaginary part of his disorder. There is reasonable medical evidence that demonstates that in one group of amphetamine addicts 43 per cent reported an 'enhanced mood' after having taken dummy tablets. and that also the combination of profound physical exhaustion and sleep deprivation (with perhaps excessive light and sound stimulation) will produce hysterical reaction experiences not unlike those reputedly otbained with hallucinogenic drugs. Glycerine on a sugar cube has not infrequently changed hands at exorbitant prices in the teenage underground and produced nevertheless the desired effect in the willing recipient.

All this is not to minimise the problem of drug misuse in the community, where in recent years it may well have reached serious proportions, but to place it in perspective in the student world. One survey (1969) carried out in three different establishments of higher education in a large city (by anonymous questionnaire and without a reliability or validity study) revealed that out of 5,000 students only 250 had ever had any experience with any 'drug', five of whom claimed to have used opiates and ten LSD. Even these conclusions must be guarded in view of the difficulty of adequate checking. Both users and non-users, however, estimated that the prevalence of drug use was far greater than was in fact shown by the survey—an essential point about this trend to exaggeration. In the USA the 'claimed' prevelance is similar, higher than is in fact shown by the reported experience of College Health Service physicians. In fact it is because drug misuse is so destructive to an academic life that it is infrequently found—the jungle law operates in that only the 'fit' survive, and the drug-users rapidly become unfit. There is an inevitable danger of complacency here, of course, in the academic community, on the grounds that because it is not our problem then there is little need for concern. Similarly, although one academic 'drop-out' means less of a problem for the campus, it inevitably means one more for the community who receives it like a dustbin, and there is little mechanism for rehabilitation. It is not without value, therefore, to consider the detailed effects of individual drugs as experienced by the more intelligent in the adolescent population, for whatever the incidence of their misuse their effects on the 'privileged' are as serious and as damaging as they can be on any developing adolescent.

Marihuana

This dried leaf may be smoked in a hand-rolled cigarette or chewed. Its taste is unpleasant when chewed, and one adolescent is reported to have said, not without humour, 'Now I know why it is called "shit".' The aroma of its smoke is sweet and sickly and readily recognisable unless the burning of joss-sticks or incense has been deliberately initiated to obscure its scent. Almost invariably it is a 'group' experience and is passed around at parties by the 'group leaders' or those who wish to impress the uninitiated. The effect on the indulger is predominantly to enhance the mood that the person is at the time experiencing—relaxation of body and mind with a degree of heightened perception of those things which the individual finds pleasant, colours, music, shapes, animals or sexual sensation. This latter may be particularly deceptive, for impotence under its use is a common male experience. In exactly the same way if a person is frightened of its use, because of its illegality or fear of what they may experience, then marihuana may well prove unpleasant for them and they express a dislike for it. They may feel sick, vomit or sweat excessively. If they persist –again in order to conform– the hallucinogenic experiences may eventually become more pleasant, but nevertheless there are more people in the student community who 'tried it once and it did nothing for me' than there are regular users. Sore and bloodshot eyes from the smoke and a persistent dry cough are signs of its regular use, but a more marked sign is that the regular use distorts the individual's critical perception of their own intellectual ability. It is a constant finding that they thought they had written a 'perfect' essay for their tutor, only to get a poor mark–and this drives them back to the solace and relief of the drug. There is no evidence of any intellectual achievement ever being better due to the influence of drugs. With a degree of inevitability they run the risk of becoming ever more regular users. It may well be, however, that only the 'side-steppers', the weaker ones and those who would be prone to seek escape and not the mastery of a setback, follow this path. With regular 'escape' comes thus the first aspect of personality deterioration–just as with the adult who cannot face the stress of an important interview situation without the 'dutch' courage of a double gin. Regular distortion of intellectual ability shows inevitably in the falling-off of academic ability–the student whose work is getting gradually worse than would be normally expected is hall-marked as one with psychological problems, in the absence of any organic disease–and drug abuse may well be that problem. Excessive use of marihuana is rare, if only because it is expensive, but occasionally it is seen and appetite suppression frequently occurs along with an almost psychotic increase in fantasy. Patients who have smoked up to 20 'reefers' a day for as long as a week or more become grossly disorientated and frequently withdraw totally from involvement with all aspects of the outside world. Vivid aggressive fantasies may be experienced and lead to bizarre forms of self-damage from the production of skin slashes with a pallette knife 'because the blood looked pretty' to drowning because 'she said she wanted to walk on the water'. The excessive and exclusive use of marihuana is as hazardous and as disorientating as is the excessive and exclusive use of alcohol–they both produce an acute psychosis. Similarly, however, both psychoses respond to the same therapy of withdrawal, although the one requires specific vitamin therapy for the alcoholism and the other tranquillisation (with such as chlorpromazine) and a 'good feed'. It is the disintegration of the critical faculties, however, that remains the danger of marihuana, which occurs, albeit temporarily, whenever it is used. Sensual pleasure is bought at the price of critical judgement, and its regular or excessive use is paid for in impairment or serious deterioration of the individual's intellect. There are many comparisons that can be made with alcohol but unfortunately with marihuana the awareness of being 'drunk' is not so precise or so specific as it is with alcohol, nor does it wear off so quickly. The body can vomit an excessive intake of drink, but its rejection of being 'turned-on' is much slower and less recognisable–hence the constant danger to the student that the work undertaken on the Sunday morning is done whilst still under the influence of what was inhaled the night before.

Stimulant Pills

Nearly every student has tried at some time some form of 'stimulant' to help him work through the night-time hours, from black coffee to cold baths. Less innocuous, however, is the attempt to remain awake with some amphetamine-like preparation, and requests for this kind of help are frequently made to university physicians. There is a serious problem here, for as was seen in Chapter Seven, a complaint of 'falling asleep' may be one of the early symptoms of depression and a self-defence withdrawal mechanism for the student who is reaching the limit of his ability to withstand a stressful situation. Stimulants to overcome this normal 'escape' physiologically will bring disaster psychologically. Similarly, the use of artificial central nervous system stimulants will enable the student to stay awake, but not to perform academically any better (if at all) than they would have done without them. Memorising ability is demonstrably diminished, physical fidgeting with an inability to sit still and read or write for any length of time ensues, and next day the effect of the physical fatigue wipes out any advantage by demanding a prolonged period of rest and recovery thus eroding the academic time even more. Amphetamines do keep people awake and initiate a feeling of alertness and self-confidence, but only for a short time, and at the cost of a relative inability to concentrate. Moreover, if used temporarily, say for a couple of hours' 'extra working' after midnight, then there is afterwards an inability to sleep so that next day is, in terms of academic production, negated in value. Their continued use produces an effect similar to anyone's experience of staying awake past the usual fatigue point–a degree of time-sense disorientation, excessive thirst and consequent frequency of urination, and other signs of cardiovascular strain with palpitations, dizziness or swollen ankles due to oedema. The effect on academic ability of continued use is accumulatively destructive, the inability to sit through an hour's lecture is accompanied by an inability to concentrate and read for as long as a whole page of a book. Confusion ensues until eventually profound exhaustion takes over and sleep demands have to be met, whereupon a sleep packed with vivid dreams and nightmares occurs. Excessive use, perhaps in large doses taken at or for a party, produces exaggeration of all these symptoms with a hang-over of excitement, physical restlessness and mental paranoia. Aggressive anti-social destructive behaviour, usually of property rather than of others or self, follows massive overdosage, and obviously when 'high' on stimulants there is an almost complete inability to intellectualise. Dependence occurs on their physical effects only, and in the student community this alone has little to offer. Because fatigue takes over and academic performance is so handicapped there is little incidence of chronic dependence; the greatest hazard to the student is mistakenly taking them before an examination because they have ill-advisedly been up all night before, working. The legend of the student who did this and under the influence of amphetamines thought he had written a brilliant paper, but had only written out his name 3,000 times, has a grain of truth in it as a depiction of the likely consequences. More frequently, however, it may be found that the student is unable to write, sit still or remain in the examination hall long enough to complete the paper, regardless of the fact that he cannot remember enough to write the answers– as a price for being kept physically 'awake' by stimulants.

The Opiates

The 'hard' drugs are those such as cocaine, heroin, morphine or other opium derivatives, which in the true terms of the definition of addiction produce a chronic intoxication, a compulsion to continue their use and a need to increase the dosage in order at first to maintain the psychological effect and eventually in order to avoid the severe physical effects of withdrawal. These addictions are totally destructive of personality and life. The average mortality after leaving hospital for the treatment of addiction to a 'hard' drug is 20 per cent in the first year, and the average death rate within five years of addiction developing is 60 per cent. 'Hard' drug addiction is suicide by inches. Methedrine, a form of amphetamine, is also– as are most of the morphine derivatives– taken intravenously, and all these agents are initially taken for the intense psychological and physical effects they produce– a sensual experience that is at first far beyond that which marihuana or any other agents produce. The 'hard' drugs, particularly heroin, are self-injected into a vein ('mainlining') or subcutaneously ('popping'), and as they are rapidly absorbed an almost immediate orgasmic sensation occurs, without any direct sexual organ involvement. This experience is a totally physical and psychological trance-like state at first and is accompanied by a feeling of warmth and flushing which gives supreme confidence—fascinated by the sensation and their thoughts they are 'high as a kite'. The initiate may experience nausea and vomiting, sweating and visual disturbances, but the addict begins to know a far more unpleasant sensation as the 'fix' wears off—the physiological symptoms of withdrawal which include an intense skin itching, dizziness, restlessness, excessive yawning and then sweating with lacrimation and catarrh formation in the nose. Twitching due to muscular spasms and cramp-like pains ensue and vomiting with diarrhoea occurs as more time passes without a dose of the opiate. The peak intensity of these 'withdrawal' symptoms occurs at the forty-eight/seventy-two hour period after a 'fix'. It is patently obvious that the continuance of an academic life as a student is incompatible with being addicted. But the misfortune is that those students who are in contact with the illegal underworld for supplies of marihuana are highly likely to meet 'pushers' who wish to increase their own income further in order to obtain more supplies of the 'hard' drugs they need—and hence initiate the weaker ones into experience with 'hard' drugs. There is a degree of social contagion to drug-taking and a malignancy that can spread—thus the maladjusted student (there are approximately three male 'hard' addicts to every one female) finding solace for his disturbance in marihuana, and selling it to others, may become also the initiate into the 'hard' market and in turn pass the contagion on once he is addicted. All drug-taking has a certain individual price, and that of true addiction demands complete academic 'drop-out', gross personality disintegration and eventually death. Furthermore, the addict, who is in all probability suffering from a personality defect that antedated the addiction anyway, becomes to the environment of the campus, a social canker.

The Major Hallucinogens

Substances derived from cactus such as mescaline, or psilocybin, do not appear as much on the European 'drug scene' as the later-developed synthetics like LSD (lysergic acid diethylamide), DMT (dimethyltryptamine), the related DET (diethyltryptamine) or STP (5-methoxy-MN-dimethyltryptamine)– all of which give the recipient a 'trip' of varying duration in which the 'mind is blown' due to the experience of major hallucination that they induce. 'Acids', as they tend to be referred to, were first explored as forms of psychiatric treatment because of the schizophrenic-like abreactions they induced, but because of their unreliability – and moreover the now well-recognised hazards of precipitating a semi-permanent psychosis – they are no longer used by the medical profession. Their illegal use, however, in the drug-taking community of the States is particularly common, although in Europe the proportion who take 'trips' is by no means as considerable.

The mind-bending of an acid trip is fraught with dangers – in the short term those of a 'bad trip' which leaves the indulger suffering from an acute psychosis marked by mental disorientation and mania, with physical lack of control characterised either by withdrawing curled up in the corner of a room, or by running about screaming and harming themselves and others. In the long term frequent trips produce a greater degree of psychological and social withdrawal from the world and retreat into their own inner world of hallucination, whilst in the excessive use of 'acid' a state akin to a catatonic schizophrenic trance is produced which may last for weeks and require semi-permanent hospitalisation afterwards, the 'mind' being truly 'blown'.

Even isolated use may be permanently harmful, for evidence is accumulating on the incidence of chromosomal damage and the longlasting psychotic after-effects which suggests that once a person has been on a 'trip' his or her personality may well be permanently impaired. The individual concerned will not appreciate that this is so, nor will the group who collectively indulge in acid-trips. Indeed, as groups those who 'turn on' tend invariably to 'drop out' from normal society as a consequence, not necessarily as a voluntary wish, and cults develop whose individual mystiques derive essentially from the hallucinogenic drugs they employ. There is, as in hard drug addiction, a certain latent predisposition in those who become 'acid-heads', and in a recent study conducted by the University of Southern California it was found that the primary quality in common amongst LSD trippers was a history of unhappy family life. The 'loner' and the 'loser' with few friends and few accomplishments is the individual particularly prone to find his or her valhalla only in the hallucinations obtained by the severe disturbance of cerebral metabolism produced by varieties of 'acid'. It is particularly obvious from all this that intellectual critical ability is the first aspect of personality to suffer—even from one 'trip'—and it follows that academic ability is progressively and perhaps permanently eroded by each experience. The use of LSD and its derivatives or analogues is incompatible with the successful pursuit of an academic career.

The detection of any drug abuse is not easy, for tutor, parent or even doctor, without a frank admission on behalf of the patient or prolonged and careful observation. Even given an admission, as was mentioned above, the claim to be a drug-user can be a distorted fantasy that is being tried-on in order to shock the adult concerned. Nevertheless, such a statement in itself indicates a lack of psychological stability on behalf of the patient and some help may be necessary. The forensic problem of proof is not easy either—cannabis or marihuana can be detected even in microscopic quantities given analytical equipment, but not biologically except in its unconsumed form. Amphetamine-taking can be proven by sophisticated urine analysis, and the hallucinogens like LSD also show breakdown products in the urine, but this too is not readily available to either doctor or teacher. Heroin or methadrine use, however, since it is taken by injection, is easily detected by a physical examination. Signs of injections, such as black and blue tatoo marks, small scabs or scars along veins on the forearm, back of the hands or lower-leg and foot are clear indications. Drops of blood on the clothing such as the shirt, sock or handkerchief are further indications, and the hard-drug addict tends to keep his sleeves rolled down to hide the marks of injections. The equipment necessary may be found and varies from the normal hypodermic syringe to the eye-dropper with items like rubber-tubing for making a tourniquet; silver paper, cotton wool, matches and a spoon are sometimes found as the apparatus used to dissolve tablets.

Such findings are obvious, but the addict can go to extreme lengths of cunning to hide his or her addiction from others– nevertheless there is one thing they cannot hide: their behaviour. Apart from being always short of money – for all types of drug-abuse are expensive– it is the personality change to those who knew him or her well before that is the most marked characteristic. Personality deterioration may be seen in apathy, intellectual disability and abrupt changes of mood from excitement to physical aggressiveness. Alternatively carelessness about personal appearance, slovenliness, bizarre appetite patterns (reefer smokers find sweets particularly appealing), unusual exclusiveness and secretive behaviour, excessive thirst and constipation are all concomitants of drug abuse– not alone but in varying combinations.

Confrontation must follow suspicion, not in terms of accusation or condemnation– and this will be based on the inadequacy of behaviour (whether it is a matter of poor academic performance or any evidence of personal disregard for society's conventions). The dirty student or the girl who wants to stay in bed all day is not normal. Failure to attend classes, persistent evidence of severe money shortage, or continual all-night parties are often suspicious signs and sooner or later the 'drop-out' will become inevitable. Psychiatric assistance at an early stage can help– given a willing attitude towards therapy. Support, continual no matter how trying and frustrating, is the only hope for the inadequate personality who is a potential or committed addict of drug-abuse. Punishment is irrelevant, because they are punishing themselves far more than society can and the privileged adolescent will inevitably surrender all privileges when he or she becomes part of the drug scene. Fortunately it happens to few, but to each one of those few it is a tragedy.

Bibliography and Further Reading

Beckett, D. (1968), *New Society*, Aug. 22.
Bewley, T. (1966), *Bull. Narcot.*, 18, (4), 1.
Binnie, H. L. (1969), 'The attitude to drugs and drug-takers of students', *Vaughan Papers*, No. 14, Dept. of Education, Leicester, UK.
Demos, G. D., and Frazer, M. P. (1968), 'Some concerns regarding drug-abuse among our youth in the USA', *Stud. Health News*, 5.
H.M. Government Report to the United Nations (1967), 'The working of the International Treaties on Narcotic Drugs', HMSO, London.
Lancet (1969), Editorial, 1, 1138.
Linken, A. (1968), 'Psycho-social aspects of Drug-taking', *Stud. Health News*, 5.
Miller, D. H. (1967), *Med. World*, Jan. 7.
—— (1969), *The Age Between*, Cornmarket–Hutchinson, London.
Observer (1970), News report, March 15, 1.
Time (1967), July 7, 12.
—— (1970), March 16, 16.
The Times, London (1970), News report, Feb. 9, 3.

CHAPTER TEN

Student Wastage

FAILURE in life is tragic, and doubly so in adolescence. One in seven of all university students in the UK fail to achieve a degree, or withdraw before examination, and as such this 13 per cent can be regarded as 'student wastage'. In the United States the figure is much higher (40 per cent), but then since entry to an American State College is, broadly, open to any high school graduate whereas in the UK only 4 per cent of young people achieve the high degree of selection necessary for university entrance, there is no strict comparison. Nevertheless, failure in adolescence to achieve committed objectives is a serious setback both to the individual and to the community, for the 4,500 students in the UK who leave university for whatever reason represent a loss of over £5,000,000 a year to the taxpayers. The underdeveloped countries can afford wastage even less, whether it be in money or in talent, and fundamentally this is the crux of the matter; whether the cause be in faulty selection, inadequate teaching or the milieu of the institution, no community can afford to waste those who have shown that in some way they are capable of further education.

Goldsmith, Johnson and Shelley were all in their day part of what is now called the problem of 'student wastage'. They all left university without a degree, one because he attacked his tutor, another for publishing an atheistic pamphlet, and the third just 'dropped out' voluntarily, but they all proved themselves in later life; and if it could be relied upon that the present-day withdrawals could do so there might be less need for concern. Unfortunately, most of the available evidence from follow-up surveys gives no such reassurance. Rather in fact does it indicate that the 'failed' student recovers only partially from the rejection process, whether it was voluntary or academic, and only then after a long 'cooling out' period of adaptation to seeking out a new career or means of employment.

Waste may take place in four ways. It may be voluntary withdrawal (more often in the first year), and the rates for women are consistently higher then those for men, or it may be due to academic failure where this sex ratio is reversed. It may be due to illness, which varies very much from college to college and country to country as the reason given (from nil to 18 per cent) but consistently affects those in the Arts and Social Studies faculties more than others, or finally and rarely, waste may be due to disciplinary action accounting for only 0·7 per cent of the total who left university in the UK (a total of 14 individuals from 43 universities)– an example of the latter being one man who shot one of the college deer! Whatever the cause, 50 per cent of all those who leave do so in, or immediately at the end of, their first year of tertiary education, and both the reasons and the effect on the individual are worthy of the most earnest perusal.

Firstly, the effect on the individual merits attention because statistics of cost or incidence are after all only figures and although annually there is some decline in the numbers (1952 overall wastage in UK, 16·7 per cent; 1955, 13·9 per cent; 1957, 14·3 per cent; 1966, 13·3 percent) the personal tragedy is not lessened because one belongs to a smaller group– indeed it may even be aggravated. The student, subject to all the normal pressures of adolescent development, physically, socially and psychologically, finds himself (or herself) away from home in all probability and starting on a path that should lead to some form of academic distinction or training for a career, only to give up or be rejected before a third of the course is completed. It may be that emotionally or socially the individual concerned never wanted to start a university or college life–nevertheless they permitted themselves to be selected and so to enjoy, even briefly, the privilege of entrance and the status of becoming a student. Whether they decide, for a variety of reasons, to give this up deliberately, or allow by reason of academic inadequacy this to be decided for them, they inevitably face a return to the environment of the ordinary community marked out as having 'failed'. Their brief university careers will have trained them for nothing–and employers are even more suspicious of the 'failure' than they are of the otherwise untested applicant straight from school. If they obtain some clerical occupation, then their colleagues who left school when they did are already trained as, say, shorthand-typists and will be ahead of them, or in a few years' time those who stayed at university will return and be appointed (because of their qualifications) as their superiors. In these ways they face constant reminders of their 'failure'. Some will deliberately seek more lowly jobs than their capabilities could normally be expected to bring and work as bus guards, delivery drivers, as shopgirls, in factories or as labourers whilst they 'cool off' from the immediate effects of their frustration. Many, finding their parental disappointment too bitter to live with, leave home and abreact socially to their middle-class background by joining the hippie-cults, sleeping rough and wandering like vagabonds from group to group of adolescent communities. These drop-outs often remain on the fringe of the student population, still eating in the student restaurants, still pretending, to themselves, to be students, and finding a bed where they can. It is from this group, who have little economic means of support apart from seasonal labouring, that many of the 'drug-pushers' arise, for drugs offer them personal relief and escape from their own dilemmas and their sale produces money to live off. Moreover, to a degree they are evasive individuals who have vacillated towards their own problems, or have personality defects that deny them either staying power or clear motivation, and these characteristics

I

are to some extent typical of the drug-taker. The ex-student is a tragic but, at times, dangerous figure. Many of the girls marry—and this in itself may well have been their reason for leaving because they were either motivated towards marriage, or else they sought it as an alternative and compensation for academic inadequacy. Other girls who seek a job find that further training is still required of them (e.g. secretarial, short-hand-typing, programming) and some reject even this and, in common with some of the men, devote themselves to what might be termed voluntary service. Child-minding, adventure playground supervising, working for agencies that care for the elderly, the handicapped, the ill-housed, the underfed or the politically underprivileged, all attract the student who failed, as if they are, by devoting themselves to such charitable enterprises, atoning for their own mistakes and doing 'something useful in society'. Rarely does the ex-student prove himself or herself with feats of great endeavour in the commercial world—perhaps because if they had the energies for that, or a strong enough motivation for personal profit, then they would not have failed anyway. More often do they become the 'chip-on-the-shoulder' types, and blame themselves, their parents, society or the university for their predicament. There is often an unchannelled bitterness which may be eruptive or smouldering and it does little to help them with adaptation. Worst of all, perhaps, is that there is no really well-organised rehabilitation service, or effective academic rescuing process for these otherwise able but poorly motivated individuals, and society is very cruel to the failure. They are placed, therefore, in a social environment that does little to help them regain self-respect, if indeed they ever had any, and the challenges they have to face are greater in fact than the ones they left behind. Truly as the community is at present geared, perhaps over-valuing academic ability and underevaluating the problems of adolescence, the failed student is found to have left the frying-pan and entered the fire.

Who is the failed student? Has he or she any specific characteristics that would lead to earlier (i.e. pre-selection) identification and so avoid the enormous personal and communal cost of wastage? Obviously a great deal of research has been done into this subject and on the broadest level many attempts have been made to identify the group, if not the individual. Firstly, and to a certain extent by way of reiteration, there are the two main types of waste–those who withdraw for personal, health or other non-academic reasons, and those who fail academically to meet the standards demanded by examination. In this latter group, of course, there are always those who, with extra time, succeed in the end. Thus, whilst in the UK in 1968 77·7 per cent of all students completed their studies and achieved their first university degree, a further 7·8 per cent did so after an extra year and 1·2 per cent after an extra two years. In all, then, 86·7 per cent of UK undergraduates graduated in 1968. Men were 76·2 per cent successful, women 81·7 per cent, and since fewer women are admitted one may presume those who are to be, in general, better academically endowed than their male colleagues–their greater success rate thus not being surprising. Of those who failed academically, an interesting variation is seen between faculties (which will be discussed in more detail below), with perhaps only one per cent failing to qualify in medicine but ten times that number failing in the biological and physical sciences. For withdrawals for other than academic reasons (but not health reasons) the Arts faculties suffered a 5 per cent loss, the Sciences 10 per cent and Architecture lost 20 per cent of its students before the final examination. This latter fact must be influenced by the alternative (and perhaps more remunerative) method of qualifying that is available to architects by way of apprenticeship. When the technologies are included a similar trend is seen where overall, without any first degree, the following percentage withdrew or failed:

	Per cent
Medicine	0·8
Social Studies	8·9
Arts	9·4
Sciences	13·8
Engineers and Technology	21·8

A combination of circumstances – from the standards of excellence demanded, to personal motivation and the 'sandwich' course of industrial worlds interfering with academic devotion – are all at play to influence these statistics.

Overseas students represent 4·8 per cent of all undergraduates in the UK, and their failure rate is higher than that of the home students (19·0 per cent compared to 13·3 per cent) with a withdrawal rate two (or three, in some colleges) times that of the indigent. However, a similar number require longer

1968	Faculty	No. of overseas students
	Engineering and Technology	582*
	Social Studies	338
	Arts	229
	Medicine	185
	Physical Science	108

* i.e. 34 per cent of all overseas students

time (7.8 per cent) to complete their studies, which speaks highly for their adaptation to all the problems they face in this country (see Chapter seven) although the failure and withdrawal rate must in many ways be blamed on these same problems.

On the more detailed level perhaps the most exhaustive analysis of 'who fails' has been carried out by Wankowski, although the best individual summary of the characteristics of the 'Student Casualty' has been published by Ryle. The syndrome of the 'disenchanted elect' was studied by means of following a cohort (all those admitted as first-year students in 1964) of 1,244 university students for three years. 1,031 got their degrees (83 per cent first time, 7 per cent with longer time) and this loss of one in ten was precisely defined. The strongest of correlations with success was that of a definite goal orientation (i.e. where the student undertook a course knowing it led to a career they wanted to follow) and the ideal of achievement of a career by means of the degree they were studying. Thus Medicine, Dentistry and Law share the fewest failures, drop-outs and wastage. The reverse was equally true in that poor goal orientation, with therefore poor motivation, led to failure or withdrawal. The survey team consisted of an educational psychologist, a psychiatrist and a records and statistics officer, and many aspects of the students' academic health were examined. The problem of stress, assessed by analysing frequency of attendance at the University Health Centre, was particularly scrutinised. The general rationale for this was that 'a learning activity which seems pointless to an unplannful person, or futile to a too compulsive planner can be tolerated for some time by both such individuals who are trying to adjust to a new environment of study. It will not, however be tolerated for too long. If the new approach to learning does not bring about a reduction of tension and if the student does not feel that his life at university is, in some way, contributing to his well-being, the prospect of reducing anxiety will seem remote. An anxiety-inducing stimulus, be it learning or an unsatisfactory social life, may become an obnoxious object, and if it cannot be avoided it might eventually lead to ill-health, or to a state of such misery that a visit to the doctors— the most obvious neutral agents at university—becomes a necessity.' This was a reasonable assumption, but the facts did not emerge with quite the hoped-for clarity. High doctor-usage was an index of those who in fact achieved a degree, but of lower standard than predicted, whilst 47 per cent of those who did well academically made frequent consultations, and 38 per cent of the poor academic students and the failures also made frequent use of the medical services. Thus, stress is common to all, with the strongest motivated having as much if not more than the lowest motivated. The problems associated with transition from school to university were, however, highlighted when the failure group were analysed, and here emerged one of the most significant features of the whole subject of 'wastage'—the 'system' is more responsible for waste than is perhaps the individual.

'Most were "crammed" at school to obtain the necessary qualifications but they are no longer subject to the discipline of a well-supervised curriculum. They are now subject to their own discipline which they have not been trained to exercise,' reported one psychiatrist considering this first year's failure group.

In the absence of immediate reinforcements, rewards, admonishments or tacit approval by teachers and other palpable consequences of learning, or in the absence of inferred satisfaction from a well-completed task, then future goal orientation and motivation becomes the most crucial factor for a student. The doctor-to-be knows that studying anatomy (which may well be repulsive to him) gets him nearer to being a doctor, the zoologist may hate dissecting the dog-fish and when he does not know what to do with his degree anyway, decides not to continue. Thus in any group of new entrants to a university, most of whom have been conditioned to a dependent and structured form of school learning, those individuals who can link their new learning to a clearer future goal have an advantage. This helps them adjust to the strange conditions of a relatively unstructured learning environment at the university and bear more easily and patiently the pain of unfamiliarity, social loneliness and academic desolation. Thus wastage is an academic problem and not in the long run a medical one. The university does not easily indulge the difficulties of the confused, compulsive or happy-go-lucky worker who is not relating his or her studies to some meaningful aspect of his or her later life. In the final analysis of first-year failure only 3 per cent failed academically, the rest of the failures 'lost interest', 'had too many social activities' or were 'haphazard' and 'not well orientated' in their work. Moreover, these students who withdrew had significantly higher school grades than those who left because they failed in the ultimate examinations. Waste, therefore, is identified with individual motivation, which in turn depends to a great extent on the whole system of tertiary education, what it offers and how it offers itself to the student.

In even greater detail, with a smaller sample, Ryle has considered the relationship of academic difficulty to psychiatric illness and concluded similarly that even with the mentally ill, personal motivation on the part of the student is the overriding feature that mitigates for or against academic success. The attitude towards achievement and towards tutors may be related to the personality of the individual, but no demonstrable difference could be found between the academically adequate and those who were having difficulty, with regard to family background, diagnostic category of psychological disorder, previous psychiatric history or treatment, clinical course of a psychological illness or family relationships. All these features had apparently no marked effect on explaining why some very disturbed students did brilliantly whilst others withdrew. It was apparent, moreover, that in most cases psychological breakdown would have occurred whether they had come to university or not – and the task of the University Health Service was in these cases detection, making arrangements for treatment and giving advice to the university and the student as to the advisability of interrupting and/or recommencing studies after recovery.

If it is not psychological illness, therefore, that is responsible for failure, but a lack of clear motiviation, what can be done about this problem? Does the fault lie in the schools, the universities or the students? To some extent the answer must be that all three share a degree of responsibility. Schools for perhaps tending to urge students to continue with tertiary education, for reasons inappropriate to the individual, universities for offering courses that accept poorly motivated students and that have inadequate counselling and vocational guidance arrangements and that are sometimes so inflexible as not to permit students to change courses easily, and students for allowing these pressures to continue because their parents want them to–they think it is a better alternative to seeking a definite career, or because it is 'what everybody else in the school form is doing'. There needs to be earlier recognition of the student with academic and motivational difficulties, and a more efficient form of academic counselling and guidance–the institution should cherish those that, by selection, they have accepted responsibility for–and there is need for constant analysis of failure patterns. Any situation where a university faculty has a regular failure rate should be investigated, for it is an intolerable waste of talent, money and personality. Certain universities persistently have lower wastage rates than others, and the personal tutorial system, the ease with which students may change from, say, medicine to music and the way in which top-class sportsmen may be nurtured academically and eventually perhaps 'given' a 'pass' degree, must all play their part in producing less 'wastage'. Academic inflexibility and obsessional objectives of 'keeping up the standards' lead to individual destruction and an intolerable waste of money. Moreover the young are rejecting these standards and these judgements of the university 'parent' are producing the 'disturbed child' syndrome just as they would in the family situation – and when it is those with higher academic talent who withdraw voluntarily, talk of 'standards' is nonsense. Withdrawal does harm the individual, and it is an act of 'academic suicide'. Nevertheless, is this not in itself a plea for help? Help – which the privileged adolescents need to enable them to overcome so many of their problems, and a plea which cannot be ignored.

Bibliography and Further Reading

Beard, R. (1970), *New Statesman*, Feb. 20, 248.

Bettelheim, B. (1950), *Love Is Not Enough*, Free Press, New York.

Coleman, T. (1967), *The Guardian*, Feb. 21.

Cumming, J. D. C. (1970), Univ. of Reading Medical Officer, Personal Communication.

Grunebaum, M. G. (1962), *Amer. J. Orthopsychiat.*, 32, 462.

Kreitman, N., *et al.* (1961), *J. ment. Sci.*, 107, 887.

Liss, E. (1940), *Amer, J. Orthopsychiat.*, 10, 123.

Marcus, I. M. (1967), in *Adolescence – Care and Counselling*, Lippincott, Philadelphia and Toronto, 94.

Pearson, G. H. J. (1954), *Psychoanalysis and the Education of the Child*, Norton, New York.

Rubinstein, B. O., *et al.* (1959), *Amer. J. Orthopsychiat.*, 29, 315.

Ryle, A., (1967) *Brit. J. Psychiat.*, 114, 755.

—— and Lunghi, M. (1968), *Brit. J. Psychiat.*, 114, 57.

—— (1969) *Student Casualties*, Allen Lane, Penguin Press, London.

University Grants Committee (1968), *Enquiry into Student Progress*, HMSO.

Usdin, G. L. (1967), *Adolescence – Care and Counselling*, Lippincott, Philadelphia and Toronto.

Wankowski, J. A. (1970), Proc. Brit. Stud. Health Assoc.

—— and Prince, R. W. (1969), Interim Report, Educational Survey Univ. of Birmingham.

Travellers' Notes

THE WORD student is almost synonymous with the word traveller these days. Many students now travel much further abroad from their native lands than ever before. There are many reasons why this should in fact be encouraged, but there are also many necessary precautions that should be undertaken before departure. It is important therefore that students travelling abroad should be properly informed. Individuals and expedition organisers are referred to the bibliography for more detailed study, but nevertheless some 'notes for travellers' are not amiss as an appendix to this book, and may in themselves prevent some of the accidents and infections that occur each year in greater and greater numbers.

(1) **Immunisation Procedures**

(*a*) Immunisation against smallpox, yellow fever, and cholera are recognised requirements for international travel. Smallpox vaccination within the previous three years is required before entry into many countries. Yellow fever inoculation during the preceding ten years is required before entering or passing through regions of Central and South America or Africa, and others designated as 'Yellow Fever Receptive Areas'.

(*b*) Yellow-fever receptive areas: The following States and territories are to be regarded as yellow-fever receptive areas under Article 70 of the International Sanitary Regulations: Aden (the Protectorate of South Arabia), Albania, Algeria, American Samoa, Antigua, Australia (that portion of the mainland north of a straight line joining Bundaberg, Queensland, to Broome, Western Australia), Bahamas, Bahrain, Barbados (except Seawell Airport), Botswana, British Solomon Islands, Brunei, Burma, Burundi, Cambodia, Cameroon, Cape Verde Islands (except São Vincent and Sal), Cayman Islands, Central African Republic, Ceylon, Chad, Comoro Islands, Congo (Brazzaville), Congo (Democratic Republic) (that part south of 10°S latitude), Cook Islands, Cuba, Cyprus, Dahomey, Dominica, Dominican Republic, Fiji, French Guiana, French Polynesia, French Somaliland (except Jibuti), Gabon, Gambia, Gilbert and Ellice Islands (except Phoenix Islands), Grenada, Guadeloupe, Guam, Guinea, Haiti, Ifni, India, Indonesia (except the Province of Irian Barat), Iran, Iraq, Ivory Coast, Jamaica, Kenya, (except the local areas of Kisumu and Nairobi airports, and of Mombasa port and airport), Kuwait, Laos, Lebanon, Liberia, Libya, Macao, Madagascar, Malawi, Malaysia, Mali, Martinique, Mauritania, Mauritius, Montserrat, Mozambique, Netherlands Antilles, New Caledonia, New Hebrides, Niger, Pacific Islands (USA Trusteeship), Pakistan, Philippines, Portugal (the Azores, except Santa Maria airport, and Madeira), Portuguese Guinea, Portuguese Timor, Puerto Rico, Qatar, Republic of Viet-Nam, Reunion, Rwanda, Ryukyu Islands, Saudi Arabia, Senegal, Seychelles Islands, Singapore, Somalia (Northern Region, except Berbera and Hargeisa), South Africa, Southern Rhodesia, South West Africa, Spain (the Canary Islands), Spanish Sahara, St-Kitts-Nevis-Anguilla, St Lucia, St Vincent, Sudan (that part north 12°N latitude), Surinam (Paramaribo and the coastal area, except Moengo, Paranam, Wageningen, the airport of Zanderij and the District of Coronie), Thailand, Togo, Tonga, Trinidad (the Counties of St Patrick and Victoria), Trucial Oman, Tunisia, Turks and Caicos Islands, Uganda, United Arab Republic, United Republic of Tanzania, United States of America (the States of Alabama, Arkansas, Florida, Georgia, Hawaii, Louisiana, Mississippi, North Carolina, South Carolina, Tennessee and that part of Texas east of a line extending from Del Rio through Wichita Fall and including those cities), Upper Volta, Virgin Islands (USA), Western Samoa, Yemen, Zambia.

(c) For travel into or through countries where cholera is endemic (India, Pakistan, Burma, etc.) immunisation against cholera within the preceding six months may be required. It may be advisable to immunise persons who intend to travel to regions with warm climates and to certain countries on the Continent of Europe against the enteric group of fevers.

(d) Procedure: Whenever possible, yellow-fever inoculation should precede smallpox vaccination, the interval being not less than four days. If primary vaccination against smallpox is carried out first, there should be an interval of twenty-one days from the date of the vaccination before yellow-fever inoculation is undertaken. Other preventive inoculations should, if possible, be avoided within three weeks of a primary smallpox vaccination.

These recommendations are precautionary; in practice it has been shown to be safe to perform several immunological procedures simultaneously.

Immunisation against cholera and the enteric fevers may be carried out at the same time as, or within four days of, yellow-fever inoculation. However, no more than two injections should be given at one session to any person except in cases of urgency. In multiple immunisations, different arms should be used.

As all 'hurried' schemes may be unsatisfactory from the immunological stand-point, longer intervals than 0–4 days between cholera, yellow-fever and TABT vaccinations should always be used when the time available permits.

(e) A short course of immunisation procedures for international travellers may be suggested as follows:

Day
1. Yellow-fever, Cholera (1), Oral Poliomyelitis vaccine.
5. Smallpox, TABT (1).

11. Cholera (2)
13. Read result of Smallpox vaccination
28. TABT (2) Oral Poliomyelitis vaccine (2)

Oral Poliomyelitis vaccine (3) should be given 4 weeks after the second dose. TABT (3) can be given some months (6) later.

(f) Validity of immunisation certificates:

1. *Cholera*–Vaccination certificates are valid for a period of six months starting six days after one injection of vaccine. One injection given before the end of the validity of the certificate renders the certificate valid for a further period of six months starting on the day of this injection. If the revaccination is recorded on a new certificate, travellers are advised to retain the old certificate for six days, until the new certificate is valid by itself.

2. *Yellow-fever* – The validity period of all international certificates of vaccination or revaccination against yellow-fever is ten years, beginning ten days after vaccination. Revaccination performed before the end of the validity of the certificate renders the certificate valid for a further period of ten years starting on the day of revaccination. If the revaccination is recorded on a new certificate, travellers are advised to retain the old certificate for ten days, until the new certificate is valid by itself.

3. *Smallpox*–Vaccination certificates are valid for a period of three years starting eight days after the date on which a successful primary vaccination is performed. In the case of a revaccination, the validity period of three years starts on the day of the revaccination.

(2) Protection of Travellers in Malaria Zones

The drugs most frequently used for prophylaxis are chloroquine, amodiaquine, proguanil and pyrimethamine. Mepacrine, which played such an important part as a suppressive agent during World War II, is now rarely used, owing to certain undesirable side-effects. Quinine is less effective for prophy-

laxis than any of the drugs above mentioned, and is not recommended unless none of these is available.

Chloroquine and amodiaquine are powerful suppressants
of all types of human malaria, and in the dosage used for prophylaxis their toxicity is low. They are inactive against the
primary tissue forms of the parasite, but will bring about
complete elimination of the parasite from the body by contin-
uous suppressive action on the blood parasites. Both drugs
are rapidly absorbed and slowly metabolised and excreted.
For many years it was thought that neither of these drugs could
provoke resistance on the part of the parasite, but in 1960 a
strain of *Plasmodium falciparum* from Colombia, South America,
was found to be resistant to both of them. More recently
similar reports have come from Brazil, Thailand, Cambodia,
and Malaya.

Proguanil and pyrimethamine are both highly active against
the primary tissue forms of *P. falciparum*, and are thus causal
prophylactics against this species of parasite. Both are effective
suppressants of all types of human malaria and both (especially
proguanil) have very low toxicity. Proguanil is rapidly
absorbed and excreted, so that for prophylaxis it must be taken
daily. Pyrimethamine is also rapidly absorbed, but is slowly
eliminated, so that sufficient concentration for malaria prophylaxis remains in the tissue for a week after ingestion of the
prescribed dose.

Both proguanil and pyrimethamine have a marked tendency
to provoke resistance, and this characteristic has been reported
from Malaya, Indonesia, New Guinea, Assam and Ghana.
Similar reports of resistance to pyrimethamine have been
received from Kenya, Tanzania, Volta Republic, Cameroon,
Nigeria, Ghana, Venezuela, New Guinea and Cambodia.
In these areas dosages of chloroquine and amodiaquine should
be used for prophylaxis. The recommended dosage would be:

Drug	Adult dose	Frequency	
Chloroquine	300 mg.	Weekly	It is not necessary to begin
Amodiaquine	400 mg.	Weekly	medication until the day
Pyrimethamine	25 mg.	Weekly	before exposure to infection,
Proguanil	100 mg.	Weekly	although in order to accustom the person at risk to the drugs, two doses before departure would be ideal.

Drug prophylaxis must be continued in all cases for at least one month and preferably two after the last day of exposure, so as to cover the period during which falciparum malaria may develop.

(3) Some Special Needs of Tropical Expeditions

(*a*) Water: In the tropics, basic requirements of water are up to ten pints per man per twenty-four hours, plus one extra pint per man per each hour's work (arduous work in extreme heat and high humidity may require twenty-five pints per man per twenty-four hours). At worst enough water should be drunk to ensure an output of at least two pints of urine per twenty-four hours. The best early indication of the urgent need to drink more water is a sudden loss of weight after sweating. One week's supply for each occupant is required per vehicle; this does not allow for the radiator to be replenished. Do not normally ration water or deliberately limit the intake. For sizeable expeditions and for those likely to skirt, let alone cross, any deserts, a large water tank is desirable. For deserts, large and small containers are required, so that, should the vehicle have to be abandoned, the small can be filled from the large, and you can walk out. For all expeditions four and a half gallon polythene containers and one litre (one and three-quarter pints) or two pints personal water bottles, preferably of metal covered with felt and with shoulder-straps, are desirable. All containers should be thoroughly cleaned with boiling water before expeditions set off.

All water for drinking, cooking and tooth cleaning, should be sterilised. Remember that water purifiers such as Halazone and iodine do not work unless there is no sediment in the water. The foreign matter will use up the Halazone and inactivate it. On a small scale, water can also be sterilised by being filtered, followed by treatment with Halazone tablets (one to a litre— one and three-quarter pints–or two pints), or with two drops of 2 per cent tincture of iodine per quart.

From the Hellespont to West Pakistan, in Africa and in South America north of Rio, swimming or paddling in fresh water should be avoided, and bathing water also sterilized, to avoid schistosomiasis (Bilharzia) which is difficult to cure: sea-bathing is free from this hazard. Avoid too much soap when bathing in hot countries.

Sterilisation can best be done by bringing water to the boil and keeping it *boiling* for five minutes.

(*b*) Salt: For the first week or two after arriving in a hot climate one or two teaspoonfuls of salt per day, extra to home needs, are required for acclimatisation. In hot countries always take some salt at all meals. Table salt is best. Take it in fruit juice or add it to the first course. Apart from this, after acclimatisation it is only necessary to add a small amount of salt to each pint, or one level teaspoonful to each gallon, of drinking water following sterilisation – immediately if feeling exhausted, when thirst requires ten to twelve pints of water per twenty-four hours to be quenched, or if you get diarrhoea. The salt should be foregone if there is not sufficient water to match it.

(*c*) Food and drink: Expeditions are advised to take all the food they can, especially protein, i.e. meat, soup and dried tinned milk, because such foods are scarce, often infected, and expensive in hot countries. Pack some supplies to make occasional attractive meals; these are of psychological value. All local meat, whether flesh, fowl or fish, and all local vegetables should be carefully chosen and prepared, and thoroughly

K

cooked. The pressure cooker kills all germs and makes tough meat more easily swallowed. Fresh fruit should be chosen with great care and melons and lettuces avoided. Dates, grapes, etc., have fragile skins and are easily infected. All fruit should be washed, wiped and peeled. Fruit from trees should also be carefully washed to remove any possible pesticide. Tea and soup are excellent 'foods' in hot countries. They are both clean and soup can be well salted and remain palatable. Local milk, ice cream and fruit juices should be avoided; bottled drinks with Western labels are safe, though the necks should be rubbed well after the tops have been removed and before the drinks are consumed. When cooling a drink, place ice outside and not inside the container. Alcohol if consumed should be taken only after sundown. Those who take, buy, prepare and cook their own food are far less likely to get ill than those who dine out. If dining out is unavoidable, well cooked hot foods should be chosen and salads rigorously avoided. Wash the hands with a hexachlorophene-impregnated soap before preparing or consuming food. Those who get 'dysentery' should not cook the food.

(*d*) Sun: Light cotton clothes are best; white clothing has been shown to reduce the solar heat load by half; so choose white or nearly white clothes to reflect the sun and keep you cool; only some can tolerate nylon, terylene or mixtures, because they tend to cause heat rash, although they are easier to maintain. Some need good sun glasses for hot countries; all require sun goggles or sun glasses for glare from deserts or snow. Two pairs of sun glasses are needed for mountaineering; tinted goggles for deserts. Suitable glasses are expensive but any type will do provided that the ultra violet rays are kept out. It the climate is very hot and dry, full loose clothes including head gear should be worn with only the face and hands out, at any rate until acclimatised. If the climate is hot and wet, short-sleeved shirts and shorts are best. In any event tan slowly every trip, expecially early on. Full clothes are also useful against flying insects after dusk and to avoid injury to the skin in scrub country and jungles. Women should pack trousers in the kit. Give your vehicle a tropical roof, i.e. two roofs, one two inches above the other, with air, which is an excellent non-conductor, between, to keep the heat out; and paint the top a glossy white, Do not drive too quickly into the heat; halt several times on the way to get acclimatised. All climates are possible without heat illness for resting man; it is work in hot or humid climates which exhausts. So avoid exercise, including vehicle maintenance, in the heat of the day; and avoid hard work for the first week in the heat while acclimatising.

GENERAL POINTS

Call on your national Consul in a large city before going to any out-of-the-way place, to find out where your nearest doctor and hospital will be.

Take your preventive anti-malarial drug regularly. Always sleep under a personal nylon or terylene mosquito net and use the net properly. Use insect repellent cream for hands and face after dusk; and keep it from eyes, nose, mouth, and plastics.

Take an extra pair of your own glasses if you are unable to see sufficiently without.

(4) Notes on the Treatment of Snake-bite

(a) Kill the snake and handle the dead snake only by the tail. Keep it.

(b) The commonest symptoms are fright and fear of death. Convincing reassurance is vital at all stages. Death from snake-bite is rare.

(c) Keep the patient at rest.

(d) Apply a lightly constricting ligature (use a handkerchief or piece of cloth to occlude veins and lymphatics draining the bitten area—but not the arteries). This must be released for one minute in every thirty.

(e) Wash the bitten surface with plain water without rubbing.

(*f*) Immobilise the bitten part as for a fracture (i.e. in a splint), and if possible keep it in a dependent position.

(*g*) Administer analgesics (e.g. aspirin) but not morphia.

(*h*) Call a doctor or transfer to hospital (with the dead snake, if available).

IN AREAS WHERE HIGHLY VENOMOUS SNAKES EXIST

The following recommendations are made on the basis that the bite is assumed to have been inflicted by a snake of a venomous species, and that basic medical facilities are available.

(*a*) By persons who have had some training but are not medically qualified:

In addition to the measures already recommended above.

(1) Administer 10–30 ml. of specific or polyvalent antivenom by the subcutaneous route, using one or more sites for injection. 1 ml. of 1:1,000 adrenaline should be injected intramuscularly at the same time to lessen the risk of anaphylaxis (allergy to the serum), and half the dose of adrenaline should be repeated 15 minutes later. The dose of antivenom may be repeated after 4 hours. Ideally, a subcutaneous trial dose of 0·2 ml. antivenom should be given and the patient observed for signs of anaphylaxis for 30 minutes before the therapeutic dose is injected. In practice the time lapse between the bite and the availability of specific treatment is usually so great that the urgency of the treatment must override the dangers of anaphylaxis. When the antivenom is given more than 8 hours after the bite, a trial dose should always be given first, since at this stage the therapeutic value of antivenom is questionable, and it would therefore not be justifiable to run the risk of an anaphylactic reaction.

(2) Give 30 mg. of prednisolone by mouth or inject 100 mg. hydrocortisone intramuscularly.

(3) Apply ice bags to the bitten part, but do *not* immerse the part in ice or ice-cold water.

(4) Maintain immobilisation of the bitten part for up to 3 days.

(5) Administer an antibiotic, preferably penicillin in large doses, e.g. 1–2 mega units.

(*b*) By a doctor: The antivenom should be given in the same dosage and with the same precautions, but by the intravenous route. The intramuscular route may be used for children or for adults with collapsed veins.

(5) General Advice for Travellers in Temperate Zones

Firstly always take out some form of insurance to cover costs of medical attention, accidents or loss of goods, and secondly select some of the 'First aid' treatments recommended below and ensure they become part of your baggage.

Food–firstly, the standard of food hygiene sold in the shops in many countries can be in parts much higher and in others much lower than what you are accustomed to. For example, in southern Europe and central America fresh fruit and vegetables may have been sprayed with insecticides and not washed, or if washed then only in non-drinking water. Certain tablets are available that can be used to treat water and render it non-infectious. It is prudent not to eat salads sold in restaurants but to buy the vegetables and wash them thoroughly in boiled water before eating them as a picnic. Fresh fruit should be peeled. Remember to clean your teeth only in treated or drinking water.

Milk is often not tuberculin tested and only occasionally pasteurised, it can be bought from farms straight from the cow and will therefore, be a hazardous food. It is wiser for campers to buy sterilised, pasteurised or tinned milk from a shop. To boil it before adding to tea or coffee is safer although to some this makes the drink unpalatable. The best of all is tinned milk.

COMMON AILMENTS

1. *Abdominal pain*–can be simply due to the unaccustomed

nature of continental food, especially when wine is taken liberally by persons unused to it. Antacids are a reliable standby and avoiding wine for 24–48 hours will frequently allow the 'abdominal crises' to settle.

2. *Abrasions and cuts*– should be well cleaned of all dirt by the use of a simple diluted disinfectant. The precaution of being immunised by injections of tetanus-toxoid cannot be over-emphasised, especially since tetanus spores are spread in animal manure, and on the continent farm animals and horse-drawn vehicles are much more common than in England, but to be effective the first two injections must be done at least six weeks before departure.

3. *Colds and 'flu*– may catch the unprepared traveller unawares and the precaution of including symptomatic remedies such as aspirin, codeine or paracetemol tablets and disposable paper handkerchieves are well worth while, since they may be handy for other purposes.

4. *Corns and rubbed feet*– are inevitable for those not used to walking long distances and extremely inconvenient. Sore feet can be rubbed with surgical spirit at night, this hardens the skin and enables it to withstand the rigours of the following day. There is no substitute for good fitting, comfortable walking shoes or boots and soft absorbent woollen socks, however, and prevention by these is wisest. Thin nylon socks do not act as a cushion nor do they absorb sweat, and if colourfully dyed they may aggravate any broken skin far from protecting it. A box of large plasters for heels. Heel protectors and a pad of lint held on by sticking tape may be invaluable. Actual corns of the toes should be encased in felt corn plasters to eliminate rubbing and abrasion. Any 'athletes' foot' infection should be cured before departure since heat and moisture will severely aggravate a latent infection. It is suggested that you consult your physicians before departure, if you suffer from this.

5. *Ear ache*– especially after swimming and after flying, can be a painful nuisance. Warm olive oil drops are a substance easily

obtained on the continent and cotton-wool plugs often alleviate. A teaspoon dipped in very hot water will soon warm, olive oil placed in the spoon will reach a comfortable temperature, and the oil can then be dropped into the ear.

6. *Diarrhoea*– the traveller's nightmare. It may be caused by an extension of the disorder diet as in (1) or by direct infection. In either case a bottle of Mist Kaolin, or else a stronger medicament, will be necessary. Treated properly and enthusiastically (the dose of Mist Kaolin should be 3 to 4 teaspoonsful every 4 hours), the ailment can be cured in 24 hour but left untreated a person can become seriously ill and may require hospitalisation, or at least incur expensive doctors' bills. The effect of ensuring that some medicine is available will be amply repaid. At the first attack avoid solid food, take fluids only for 24 hours or so, and the medicine. A rapid cure ensures when prompt action is taken.

7. *Fever*– feeling ill and off colour can be transient and may be due to a variety of self-limiting conditions; a true fever lasting 24 hours or more indicates the need for medical aid, so investment in a clinical thermometer is advisable for any parties.

8. *Insect bites and stings*– Mosquitos, ant and horse-flies are bigger and more vicious the further south one travels. For both men and women an insect repellent is advisable. Once bitten the danger is of infection by scratching. An anti-histamine cream or aerosol will relieve much of the irritation, and treat jellyfish stings liberally with anti-histamine applications.

9. *Muscular strains and cramps*– Climbing and long walks, especially if carrying heavy rucksacks, inevitably produce sore muscles, but a torn muscle or severe strain will be eased considerably by the massage that is necessary when you use a linament. Common remedies such as linaments do a lot to ease the pain or discomfort of an aching shoulder or calf. Cramp is dangerous and everyone is aware of the hazard of swimming soon after a large meal, but one particular aspect of

hot climates is worthy of mention, namely salt loss through sweating. It is a good tip to take plenty of salt at every opportunity with meals and the picnic pack should always contain a packet of ordinary table salt.

10. *Over-indulgence*—in wine and alcohol will bring just retribution. A popular continental remedy for the hangover is Fernet-Branca, obtainable in all bars. It is bitter and unpleasant, but effective in dispelling the near-death feeling next morning.

11. *Pain*—from any cause can strike unawares. It would be foolhardy not to include a bottle of an analgesic in the rucksack.

12. *Prickly heat*—is an irritation of the skin due to blocked sweat glands, blocked either by sun-burn creams or talcum, and is relieved by the application of surgical spirit, after-shave lotion, or calamine, which dissolves the plugs in the pores, or soothes the itch.

13. *Seasickness*—the pharmacist can offer a wide variety of specific preventions but often merely by staying on deck and not laying into the duty-free liquor in the stuffy below-decks bar is a sensible prevention. Any drug, to be effective, must be taken at least one hour before sailing time.

14. *Sprains*—a sprained ankle for a hiker is ruinous, but the provision of either a 3 in wide elastoplast bandage or a crepe bandage will save the day. Of course, boots are necessary and the foolish who undertake cross-country hikes in sandals deserve their mishaps. Nevertheless, a sprain should be firmly strapped up to support the injured joint and if it swells, then this can be relieved by alternate warm and cold water bathes, or often the simple cold water (mountain stream) compress, i.e. a pad of linen soaked and wrapped around the joint, eases considerably the discomfort and swelling.

15. *Sunburn*—must be preveted. Oils in the long run are cheaper than creams, or aerosol packs but all these may be cheaper abroad. They must be used liberally and frequently with repeated application after each bathe, and the sunbather

should time his or her exposure to start with 30 minutes on the first day, increasing gradually. If you exceed this you will suffer unbearably. Fair-haired and ginger-haired people generally tan badly and burn easily, nylon shirts and blouses do not prevent sun-burn as nylon permits the passage of ultra-violet rays. The underneath parts of chins, arms and body should be equally protected on the beach or in snow, since the rays are reflected upwards by sand or snow. If a burn is sustained then wet-dressings with vinegar, i.e. pieces of gauze dipped into a saucer of vinegar and applied direct to the affected area, will ease and encourage healing, or calamine lotion, applied in moderation is an alternative. Do not pick off peeling skin or pop blisters—skin, dead or alive, offers its own protection to the newly-forming tissues underneath.

16. *Sunstroke and heat stroke*—affects as a sick dizzy headache and dry burning skin. Aspirin, cool shade, drinks of innocuous quality such as peppermint tea infusions or fruit juices, or salty water and bathing of the skin and forehead with a flannel soaked in cold water often suffice to produce recovery. Salt intake as mentioned above is one precaution; sensible gradual exposure and the consumption of liberal drinks of innocent fluids and fruits such as melons or peaches are other precautions. The bottle of mineral water is a better provision than a litre of wine for the mid-day picnic in the hot south. Like Somerset Maugham's characters, save the liquor till after sundown.

17. *Tooth cavity*—a filling may come loose whilst abroad and a small stick of Gutta-Percha may be bought which is like chewing gum and makes a useful temporary stop to enable you to wait for your return home for permanent repair.

Finally, a word about sanitary arrangements. Toilets abroad may not be the best in the world and a toilet roll is a useful commodity to take. For the female a stock of their usual menstrual protection is necessary; foreign ones are often primitive, or in remote areas even unobtainable.

Good luck on your journey – sensible preparation saves much later discomfort.

Bibliography and Further Reading

Adam, A. (1966), *A Travellers' Guide to Health*, Hodder and Stoughton, London.

Covell, G. (1968), 'Malarial Prophylaxis', *Prescrib. Journ.*, HMSO, London.

Trans. Roy. Trop. Med. and Hyg. (1962), 56, (1), 93.

World Health Organisation (1967), *Vaccination Certificate Requirements for International Travel*, Geneva.

Index